Allan Kardec Educational Society
P.O. Box 26336
Philadelphia   PA 19141
Phone (215) 3294010
http://www.allan-kardec.org

Original Title: E A Vida Continua (FEB – Federação Espirita Brasileira)
Translation copyright © Allan Kardec Educational Society, 2000

Cover and book design by Kevin Kall

Manufactured in the United States of America
First print: October, 2000.

Library of Congress Catalog Card Number 00 134848

Xavier, Francisco C.
And Life Goes On

ISBN 0-9649907-3-3

CONTENTS

The Translation of *And Life Goes On…*:
Our Guiding Principles iii
Introduction vii
Emmanuel's Preface xi
Chapter 1—An Unexpected Encounter 1
Chapter 2—On Friendship's Doorstep 9
Chapter 3—Friendly Agreement 17
Chapter 4—Renovation 25
Chapter 5—Meeting Again 35
Chapter 6—Empathy 45
Chapter 7—Alzira Breaks The News 55
Chapter 8—Cultural meeting 63
Chapter 9—Brother Claude 73
Chapter 10—Evelyn Serpa 83
Chapter 11—Ernest Fantini 93
Chapter 12—Judgment and Love 103
Chapter 13—New Tasks 113
Chapter 14—New Directions 125
Chapter 15—Moments of Analysis 137
Chapter 16—Revitalizing Work 147
Chapter 17—Matters of the Heart 155
Chapter 18—The Return 163
Chapter 19—Life's Revisions 177
Chapter 20—Plot Discovered 189
Chapter 21—Return to the Past 201

Chapter 22—The Basis For a New Future 213
Chapter 23—Ernest in Service 225
Chapter 24—Evelyn in Action 239
Chapter 25—New Directives 253
Chapter 26—And life goes on 263
About The Writer—Francisco C. Xavier 281

THE TRANSLATION OF
AND LIFE GOES ON...:
OUR GUIDING PRINCIPLES

Sensus non verba (Meaning not words)
Cicero

The Translation and Editorial Team has seen the challenge of translating *And Life Goes On...* from its original Portuguese in two ways. We might best describe them metaphorically.

Imagine that two individuals have been invited to give the same talk to different audiences. The first speaker takes the theme to heart, delves into its ideas, convinces himself of its facts, and when on stage, speaks with a profound conviction, allowing his audience to share in his emotions to the extent that it enthusiastically affirms every major point, and endorses his conclusions. This audience is captivated by the ideas, applauds warmly, and avidly seeks to learn more from the speaker during the break.

The second speaker delivers basically the same speech—where content is concerned—but uses a methodical approach, lacks humor and feeling, and speaks in a monotone. The audience stays to the end, applauds respectfully, and quietly heads for the exits.

Always our challenge has been to make sure that the audience for *And Life Goes On...*, which will come hoping for the first kind of experience, will not find itself surprised—and disappointed—by the second kind. Both presentations may be correct in their details; only one is memorable.

Thus, from the outset we sought to deliver an experience like our first example, one wherein the book's emotions, expressions, attitudes, and personalities would have the same liveliness, power, and meaning for modern American readers as the original work had for its Brazilian ones. This was particularly critical in the reproduction of dialogue. Here we wanted to carry over the tension, rhythm, and flow of the original Portuguese into English idioms—a task that demanded a good deal of creativity since differences in grammatical structure and levels of precision between Portuguese and English are often dramatic. Further, we sought to recreate the dialogues in a way that reflected both the spoken language of contemporary America and at the same time maintained the high literary quality that marks the best currently read books in this country.

The difficulties of such an enterprise are the same that have confronted literary translators since Cicero and Quintilian, and have concerned those who have written about the art and theory of translation for over two thousand years. The approach we chose decidedly avoided the literal, strict word-for-word matching, or the other extreme, that of adaptation or free interpretation. Instead, we embraced what Dryden established as the high road and called *paraphrase*, 'or (the process of) translation with latitude, where the author is kept in view by the translator, so as never to be lost, but his words are not so strictly followed as his sense, and that too is admitted to be amplified, but not altered'[1].

Thus, we have tried in these pages to eliminate anything that by its cultural and linguistic particularity would create a barrier between our American readers and the book's message. The content is completely faithful to the ideas and observations of André Luiz, as he communicated them in the 1960s; we hope that the reader will find, however, that this work speaks directly to his or her soul today in an unaffected manner that avoids the stylistic stiffness of much translated work. We wanted to offer you a book as André Luiz might have written it had he been writing in English –a book that would evoke in the American reader the same feelings of reverence, faith, and spiritual comfort experienced by the readers of the original. This, we believe, is that book.

This is *not*, then, the work of translators in the strictest sense of the word, but our expression of a powerful experience by inspired writers and poetic souls. We hope you enjoy the experience.

The Editorial Team

---

[1] *Cited in George Steiner,* After Babel: Aspects of Language and Translation *(Oxford University Press, 1998), p. 269. For a full discussion of Dryden's position the author makes reference to W. Frost,* Dryden and the Art of Translation *(Yale University Press, 1955).*

INTRODUCTION

The dawn of a new century is upon us and, as we review the connections that bind us to the past, we try to learn from our mistakes and at the same time put together the pieces of the puzzle of life. It is only when we come to understand how they all fit that we will be able to look ahead to the future, fully aware of our own responsibility for the consequences of our actions.

Physics long ago proved to us that within the cosmic universe there is a reaction to every action. We, as an intrinsic part of the universe, are subject to its natural laws. Consequently each of us will experience the results of our actions. It is not difficult for us to see the results of greed, selfishness, and pride through the ages. Somehow the story seems to repeat itself, although with different characters, scenes, and plots. We still stifle noble ideas, embrace destruction, and postpone a truly moral way of life.

The story from *And Life Goes On* takes us on a journey from life on Earth to life in the spiritual realm. In this fascinating novel, two strangers, Evelyn and Ernest, meet during their final days on earth. When they encounter each other again in the spiritual plane, they come to realize that their lives have been interrelated and are part of a much larger picture. By helping their loved ones on earth to overcome their difficulties and correct some of their mistakes, they discover new dimensions of feeling and awareness. This is an inspiring story, which demonstrates the inescapable law of action and reaction.

This novel, the last one in a collection of sixteen books authored by André Luiz, has been brought to us through the paranormal gifts of Francisco C. Xavier (1910 -). *And Life Goes On* was originally written in Portuguese and first translated by Marcelo de Almeida. The initial draft has since undergone countless revisions by a large editorial team. Many have volunteered their time and energy along the way, contributing with various readings, detailed revisions, and careful research. To them, and in particular to Eline Anders, Antulio Bomfim, Etelvino Cyriaco, Carmen Cuming, Elza d'Agosto, Andrea Dessen, Brenda Haney, Maria 'Ju' Hanna, Anne Jamieson, Ily Reis, Maria Sulli, and Stan Thomas, our sincere appreciation. Dr. Robert Champ, once again, offered his expertise, editing the original translation and "miraculously" adding life and color to the book. A special thanks goes to Dr. John Zerio, who has wholeheartedly dedicated not only his time and effort, but his soul to keep us focused and united during the entire project. We also thank FEB's (Federação Espirita Brasileira) president, Mr. Juvanir B. Souza, for his unconditional support of this endeavor. Above all, we thank the Creator and the "spiritual ministers" who have patiently guided all of us in this work.

It is our intention that this book will be pleasant to read and, above all, will inspire you to reflect. We hope that it will offer you an opportunity to realize that what we are now is a result of our past, and what we will be tomorrow is a reflection of our present! We hope you will take the time to stop and think, and to make that difficult inner voyage that will unveil the true self, the one bereft of all the masks and disguises created through time in order to portray a pleasing image. Once conscious of this inner reality, creating positive change becomes a challenging task but a most rewarding one. Only when we realize this will each one of us reap the benefits of our deeds, and the world experience a true change. When this happens, the inevitable ensuing happiness will break the long dark cycle of tears and suffering and lead to a better life for all who search for growth. If this work has shed some light on your path and given you, in any way, a new perspective on life, we believe that this project will have been a success. If you would like to share your thoughts with us, please write to us at AKES or visit our web site: http://www.allan-kardec.org.

Jeanne and Paul Murphy
Project Directors
October 3, 2000

EMMANUEL'S PREFACE

Dear Reader:

We are not writing this to introduce André Luiz to you, or to exalt his name. From the Spirit Realm, this friend has earned our affection and gratitude for the many remarkable books he has already dictated, filling his readers with hope and spiritual wisdom. In this volume, it is fair to say, André Luiz offers insights into aspects of the life-after-life different from those covered in his early book, *Nosso Lar – A Spiritual Home*, named after the community in which he found himself after his passing.[2]

All the characters in the current tale are authentic, though their names have been changed to avoid harming loved ones on Earth. While it is true that the way their personal stories unfold is quite different from André Luiz's own, we should note that such experiences depend on the levels of knowledge and responsibility of each individual, and that these vary ad infinitum. Indeed, life in the spirit realm has a wealth of facets,

---

[2] *Translator's Note: Nosso Lar – in Portuguese 'Our Home.' The book was published in the United States with the title "Nosso Lar – A Spiritual Home," by AKES – Allan Kardec Educational Society, Philadelphia, PA.*

and one's experiences are invariably connected with one's state of mind in ways that are perfectly logical. For instance, the greater the intellectual preparation of an individual, the more painful the results of wasted time are. Likewise, the more rebellious one is before the Truth, the more severe the consequences of one's stubbornness will be. Besides, we must consider that the social organization that exists in the next realm is shaped by individualities that still exhibit the mental conditioning of the habits they acquired or cherished on Earth. As such, a person who lived her entire earthly life in an Asian setting will not find, on entering the spirit realm, the social organization and construction forms of a Western community and vice-versa. The Divine Plan that guides the workings of the Universe supposes neither sudden nor violent transitions. In fact, time and spirit of service are the sustainers of every worthwhile enterprise in the higher realm.

Not to prolong this introduction with unneeded commentary, we simply want to reaffirm that here we find, after the Great Transformation, our own spiritual portraits framed by the situations we have created, rewarding us for the good we have produced or demanding correction for the evil we have bred.

Let us therefore savor this book by André Luiz, assured that we will find in its pages many pieces of our personal history as gentle invitations to meditation and self-analysis. We learn here that life goes on, bursting with hope and opportunities to serve, with progress and accomplishments, in all the districts of Cosmic Life, bound by the laws of God.

Emmanuel[3]

Uberaba, April 18, 1968

---

[3] *Translator's Note: Emmanuel is Francisco C. Xavier's spiritual guide.*

Chapter 1

AN UNEXPECTED ENCOUNTER

The wind was playing among the dried leaves of the trees when Evelyn Serpa decided to sit down on the park bench, which had seemed almost to invite her to stop and rest. In the small, flower-filled park around her all was quiet. Although the October afternoon was warm, few tourists were visiting the mineral springs that day. Evelyn, while among them, was by herself. Her personal assistant, who had come with her to the resort, had remained at the hotel.

The turbulence at home was far behind her now. She had fled it, longing for solitude, wanting to think—which was exactly what she was doing here at the moment hiding under the green shelter of the trees, staring out at the small rows of blooming azaleas that announced, in vivid color, the coming of spring. She felt comfortable and at ease for once. Settled on the bench, with only the thick foliage close around her, she gave her thoughts free rein for the first time since her arrival, letting them wander where they would.

Back home, her doctor—a kindly man—had recommended that she try to build up her strength and get as much rest as possible. Once she returned from the spa, surgery awaited her, and she would need all the strength she could muster to hold up under it. The risks and advantages of the dreaded operation had preyed on her mind constantly. But today, for some reason, her thoughts led her in another direction—toward the memories of her short existence; and these, once started, came back to her mind in ever stronger currents.

She had married six years earlier, and in the beginning everything had been like a voyage on a cruise ship plying calm blue waters. She had a husband she loved and who loved her. She was happy. In the second year of the marriage she became pregnant. Both she and Caio had waited for the birth of their child eagerly. But the pregnancy also brought sickness. Her body, she discovered, wasn't responding in the normal way. Her kidneys were incapable of withstanding the smallest strain, and her heart seemed like a motor always on the verge of sputtering to a stop. The gynecologists that she consulted recommended a therapeutic abortion. Grieved, the couple talked the matter over, and, finally, despite overwhelming sadness at the loss, they had consented. The infant was snatched from Evelyn's womb like a chick stolen from its nest.

After that, life's journey became choppy indeed. The calm waters turned into a sea of tears. Caio underwent a metamorphosis. He became simply a friend to her, always civil and concerned but without showing the slightest romantic interest. Soon he was carrying on an affair with a single, unattached young woman, whose intelligence and liveliness Evelyn could sense from the little notes—full of passionate phrases and pink kisses—that she often found in the the pockets of the forgetful Caio.

At home, she felt abandoned, disenchanted, and perhaps it was these feelings more than anything else that set off the periodic attacks of chest pain she began to experience. During the attacks, she became nauseated and had excruciating migraines. Her hands and feet turned alternately hot and cold, and her blood pressure became alarmingly high. At the height of an attack she felt as if she were going to die. Then for some reason she would get better, at least for a time, only to relapse—falling into the same pattern after every argument with her husband.

The attacks had quickly sapped her resistance, and now her strength was waning. For over two years she had seen all kinds of specialists. The verdict was unanimous. Only a very delicate surgical procedure would cure her. Listening to the doctors, she felt, deep down, that her physical problem was very serious indeed, perhaps fatal. "But," as she often asked herself, "who really knows?" At the moment she was listening only to the chirping of some nearby sparrows, a welcome musical background to her thoughts.

Suddenly, though, she found herself reviewing her

own life, making a list of her aspirations and failures. Should she avoid the risks of a difficult surgery and remain sick even if that meant she had to live with a man who had already begun to disrespect her in her own home? Would it be more reasonable to accept the help medical science was offering, get back her health, and build a new life—just in case her husband abandoned her for good? At twenty-six, didn't she deserve a new chance at future happiness? How she would love to talk to her natural father right now! She missed him so much. He had passed away when she was still very young, and she had grown up an only child protected by a tender, caring mother, whose second marriage had brought into her life a good-natured and attentive stepfather. Along with her husband, they were her family back home.

Fanned by the afternoon breeze, Evelyn brought each in turn—husband, mother, stepfather—before her mind's eye.

Then, without warning, the images of her father and the baby she had been forced to abort came to her vividly. She was a religious woman, a practicing Catholic, and she believed, where life after death was concerned, in the notions instilled in her by her faith. Yet she couldn't help thinking to herself, "Where are my father and baby now? If I die from this disease, will I meet them? Where? But—is it really right to think about such things with the thought of my own death always on my mind?"

Evelyn was actively engaged in this self-questioning when she became aware of someone standing directly in front of her. He was a mature gentleman, and he was smiling at her in a friendly way which, after her initial surprise, inspired both curiosity and a certain admiration.

"Mrs. Serpa?" His tone was full of respect. She nodded yes, but didn't quite manage to hide her embarrassment at being approached by the man.

"Please forgive me," he continued, "but I hear you live in São Paulo.[4] I live there, too. A mutual acquaintance of ours has told me that we have—a common problem."

"A common problem? I'm sorry to hear it," she replied. She noted his own embarrassment, and spoke these words in the friendliest tone she could manage.

Encouraged, the man introduced himself. "Don't be frightened, Mrs. Serpa," he said. "I'm Ernest Fantini."

"Glad to meet you," Evelyn replied simply. The man's face, she saw, was deeply lined. He seemed, by his stance, movement, and color, to have been weakened by some wasting illness. "Sit with me and relax for a while," she invited him. "This is an enormous park, but it seems we're the only ones interested in taking advantage of it."

Ernest Fantini settled on a nearby bench and, more encouraged than ever, restarted the conversation in what was quickly becoming a growing mutual sympathy.

---

[4] Translator's Note: São Paulo - the largest city in southern Brazil and capital of the state with the same name.

"I heard about your illness through the owner of the hotel. Yes, we're both staying there. She's friendly with your personal assistant, and I learned through her that you're also going to have the operation. "

"Also?"

"That's right. We seem to have the same medical problem."

"Really?"

"Yes, my blood pressure goes wild at times," he explained. "My body seems to work just fine one day, then the next it goes to pieces. I've been going to specialists for three years now. Just recently they've given me even worse news: X-rays show a tumor in my adrenal gland. I'm afraid I'm in for some hard times."

"I see, " said Evelyn, paling slightly at this news. "I know all about the disease you're describing. You don't have to tell me anything about it. Every now and then you have an attack. You feel like you're suffocating, your heart beats out of control, your stomach aches, your head aches, your neck veins swell, you have cold and hot flashes at the same time, and you start thinking you're about to die."

"Yes, yes, that's it!"

"Then you seem to improve, but the moment you get upset, the whole thing starts all over again."

"I see that you do know all about it."

"Yes, unfortunately."

"My doctor told me the name of it a few times, and I'd like to know if you recognize it."

Ernest took a small notebook out of his pocket and

read aloud from it the exact word that defined their illness. Evelyn could hardly hide her distaste for the scientific term. Nonetheless, she took hold of herself. "Yes," she replied, "my husband told me our doctor had made the same diagnosis in my case."

Ernest noticed how uneasy she had suddenly become, and tried to be of better cheer: "It's all right, Mrs. Serpa, at least it's a disease with a rare and beautiful name."

"Which doesn't stop it from giving us attacks," Evelyn retorted, though with a smile on her lips. "Frequent and ugly ones, too."

Ernest had no immediate response to this sally. Instead he stared up at the blue afternoon sky, as if trying to find in it some hint as to how he could elevate the conversation to another, more agreeable level. For her part, Evelyn accepted this pause. She sat in silence, too, moved by her new friend's condition, and wondering, like him, how she could change the topic and move on to something of a finer nature. In his presence, she found herself anxious to reflect, to philosophize, and most of all, to forget all about the subject of suffering.

Chapter 2

ON FRIENDSHIP'S DOORSTEP

On the road not far away from them, a small horse-drawn carriage appeared, moving very slowly in their direction. Watching it close in the distance, Ernest said, "I understand you might be tired, but if you'd like a ride around the spa—."

"Oh no, thanks, I really can't," Evelyn returned. "Rest is my best therapy now."

"Of course. Bumpy rides aren't good for people in our condition."

Finally, after what seemed like an interminably long time, the carriage passed them, and only then did they discover the reason for its slow pace. Clearly it must have been in an accident of some sort; one of the wheels was broken, making any movement faster than a walker's pace impossible. The young coachman, on foot himself, was guiding his horse gently along, giving it almost free rein to move onward.

Evelyn and her friend followed the carriage with

their eyes until it disappeared around the next corner.

With a wide smile, Ernest said calmly, "Mrs. Serpa...."

"Oh, call me Evelyn," she interrupted, returning the smile with a wide, frank one of her own. "I think that since we're joined by this rare disease, we have the right to a little spontaneous familiarity. Don't you?"

"All right, then!" he returned, happily. "And please call me Ernest from now on."

He laid his pale hand on the back of the long bench and continued, "Evelyn, have you ever read any metaphysical literature?"

"No, Ernest."

"Well, let me tell you that this little carriage that we just saw reminds me of a few ideas I came across in my reading yesterday. I've been studying the work of a gifted author, and he says in one of his definitions, which he thinks only scratches the surface of the matter, that a human being is like that carriage, horse, and coachman; the three of them work together."

"How can that be?" Evelyn was a little taken back by the metaphor. She glanced at her new friend with brilliant, mocking eyes.

"Well, the carriage is equivalent to the physical body," he replied. "The horse can be compared to the spiritual body, the supporter and mainstay of our physical lives. The coachman symbolizes our own spirit—in other words, the mental part that governs our actions. Now, a damaged carriage, like the one we just saw, is like a sick body. Once it's broken down and useless, the coachman eventually gets rid of it—tosses it on nature's scrap heap, so to speak—and goes on with his work. This process could be described as the process of death. He rides on his horse anyway, though, and together they keep making steady progress. Do you see the analogy? The physical body, from the moment we can't use it any more, goes back to the ground that it came from. The spirit, on the other hand, has its own body, made of a subtler matter which, incidentally, conditions our earthly existence. The spirit then starts to live in this spirit-body, in another plane where the old body, which is made of comparatively dense matter, would be worthless. . ."

Evelyn laughed. Not wanting to seem disrespectful, however, she said, "A clever theory, Ernest! You talk about death very well. But what happens to this trio during sleep?"

"We can reasonably assume that during physical sleep all three elements rest. The quality of rest varies from coachman to coachman—that is, from spirit to spirit. When we sleep, the heavy carriage or material body always rests, but the behavior of individual spirits differs considerably. For instance, after a heavy meal for the coachman and horse, neither of them is able to move, in which case the carriage doesn't move either. But if the coachman is in the habit of studying and doing good works, he will, while the carriage is undergoing repairs and readjustments in the coachhouse, use the horse to go on educational trips or take up some other task. On the other hand, if the coachman is unskilled and inexperienced, and afraid to go on trips, then every time the carriage needs fixing, he'll stay near the coachhouse and wait there for the repairs to be finished. Then he'll take the carriage back, just as if it were armor for his own defense."

Evelyn threw up her hands in a gesture of disbelief at this explanation. "I'm afraid I don't know anything at all about these metaphysical notions," she said.

"Do you follow any religion in particular?"

"Yes, I do. I'm a Catholic—not a fanatic, mind you, but I try hard to live according to the tenets of the faith. I believe in the Church's teachings, and I follow them as well as I can."

"You deserve a lot of credit, then. Every firm conviction is honorable. I envy you for your perfect trust."

"Aren't you religious, Ernest?"

"I wish I were. I'm a seeker of truth, really; a free thinker—a freelance sniper on the battlefield of ideas, you might say."

"Then you're reading about metaphysics just to entertain yourself?"

"Entertain myself? Oh, no! I'm reading out of necessity. Are you forgetting, Evelyn? We're both about to undergo surgery that could be fatal. Maybe our luggage is being packed right now for the *long trip!*"

"From which no traveler returns," Evelyn added.

"Who knows."

"I see," said Evelyn, smiling. "So you're studying metaphysics like a traveler who's off to a foreign country—to learn all about its currency, language, customs, fashions. You're taking the crash course, getting concise information—that kind of thing."

"Well, I can't deny it. Nowadays, I have a lot of extra time on my hands and I use it, as much as possible, to study everything I can find relating to the sciences of the soul. I'm especially interested in references to the survival of spirits, who are supposed to continue their lives on other planes. And, of course, I'm also interested in learning about communicating with them."

"And have you found any proof that these communications can really take place? Have you gotten any direct messages from your loved ones on the other side?"

"Not yet."

"And this doesn't discourage you?"

"Not in the least."

"Well, frankly," said Evelyn, feeling skeptical and grateful at once. "I prefer my own beliefs. They give me confidence without doubt, prayer without all the mental torture."

"Then your inner state is a blessing and I'm glad with all my heart that your religion makes you happy. But what if life on a different plane *is* in our future? And what if questions about it happen by chance to pop into your mind?"

"Ernest, how can you say that when you don't have one iota of proof that the soul survives in the state you're talking about?"

"But I can't disbelieve the proofs offered by great teachers and other people of the highest moral character who have had it demonstrated for them."

"Well, then," Evelyn returned, in good humor, "you

keep your researchers and I'll stay with my saints."

"I don't object to that arrangement at all," Ernest replied in a similar mood, "especially considering all the excellent lawyers you have.[5] But I do have a real thirst for knowledge, Evelyn, and I can't give it up. Before I got sick, I was so sure of myself. I was in command of every situation, even if I didn't know one body organ from the next. But a tumor in your adrenal gland isn't just a pebble in your shoe. It's something like seeing a ghost—it's an omen that something serious is going to happen. It forces you to think, to meditate, to analyze."

"Are you afraid of death?" Evelyn asked once again in a rallying but more delicate tone.

"Not really. How about you?"

"Well, I don't want to die. I have my parents, my husband, my friends. I love life, but—"

"But?"

"If God decides my life has to end, I'll accept it."

"And you don't have any problems with that? Doesn't your conscience ever bother you?"

"Oh, so now you're going to start examining my conscience, are you," she said, laughing. "I had to do that in the confessional already." Then she added, "I have to say, though, that the evil others do to us is part of the expiation of our sins before God. Our own evil

---

[5] *Translator's Note: Something of a telling joke. He is saying not only that priests would have good arguments to which he would have a hard time objecting but, in the spirit of raillery that characterizes the conversation at this point, referring to priests as casuists, that is, those who, like lawyers, argue from specific cases and not necessarily from principle.*

acts are like punches we give ourselves—that's the way I think of it anyway. So I try to keep watch over myself. I know that I must not harm anyone. And in confession I find the medicine that helps immunize me against it, and that keeps my inferior tendencies from taking over. I don't want to spend too much time beating myself up, you know."

At this statement of the case, Ernest looked on with amused admiration. "Really, it's remarkable, Evelyn, how an intelligence like yours has adapted itself with such gusto and sincerity to confession."

"Of course, I also have to know the priest I'm confessing to," she continued. "I don't want to buy a ticket to Paradise by pretending to have qualities I don't. I do, though, want to work to correct the faults I have. So I can't open my heart to just anyone—to someone who can't understand me or who wouldn't be of any help."

"I see."

Evelyn's tone now became more serious and her voice a little more trusting. "Believe me," she said, "I've been living much more carefully myself since my illness. The day before coming to the spa here, I went to confession. And I can even tell you what my old confessor and I talked about."

"Oh, no, no! I don't think you should." Ernest stammered out the words. He was surprised at the devotion and generosity of spirit with which Evelyn expressed herself.

"Why not? We're here talking just like friends who have known each other for ages. You mention your preparations in the face of possible death—then you won't let me describe mine? Really, Ernest!"

Both of them laughed openly, and in the pause that followed, their eyes met, turning a mere chance glance into a gaze with meaning neither of them could mistake. Their faces reflected a sudden note of surprise. The gaze made them realize how far they had come in the past few minutes toward a much closer intimacy.

Where have I seen this young lady before? Ernest asked himself, feeling a little dizzy. *She's so beautiful, so intelligent.*

Where could I have seen him? she thought, *Such a mature man, so bright and sympathetic and so full of understanding!* And she found that she couldn't, for the life of her, suppress the pleasant sense now overwhelming her.

The interval nonetheless proved somewhat unsettling for both of them. By now twilight had descended on them, with its growing dark colors and shadows. Evening had arrived.

Chapter 3

FRIENDLY AGREEMENT

E rnest noted how flustered Evelyn was by his gaze and tried to calm her down. "Let's go on with our talk, Evelyn," he said. "Please, don't let my presence make you uncomfortable. Try to see me with your mind instead of your heart. I'm a sick man, old enough to be your father, and believe me when I say that I think of you as a daughter." His voice faded somewhat, but he shortly recovered his strength and finished the thought, "—the daughter I wish I had instead of the one I do have."

There was, Evelyn realized, much inner suffering behind these words. She decided to change her approach emotionally. "You wouldn't be happy with a daughter as sick as I am," she assured him. "But let's go back to my problem—the confession situation."

"Don't tell me any sad stories, though—please," he pleaded in a teasing tone.

"All right, I won't," she continued, smiling. "We

don't have much time for stories, anyway. But since we're talking so openly like this, Ernest, and in a place that might be a hallway into the beyond for one of us, I want to tell you there's only one thing that upsets me. I've had my disappointments, just like everyone else. My father died before I was two years old, and my mother married not long after. When I was still practically a baby, I started going to a Catholic boarding school, and after that, I got married. My husband wasn't much like the man I had dreamed about, unfortunately. But the worst of it is that in the middle of our romance a tragedy happened: a young man—a fine, honorable boy—killed himself because of me. This was six months before my marriage. Before he succeeded that last time, he had tried committing suicide once before, when he saw I was on the verge of rejecting him. I felt so sorry for him. I tried to reconcile with him, or at least console him, but it wasn't any use. My feelings kept bouncing back and forth between him and the man I married, and when he saw the situation, he couldn't stand it. He shot himself through the heart. Ever since then, any happiness I've had has been tainted. Everything I feel and do is touched by both lights and shadows. And you know—it's sad— even though I give all the love I have to my husband, I've never been able to become a mother. So you see, I live a sad life. So frustrated, so weak."

"Now, now," Ernest chided her softly. He thought for a moment, searching around for words that would put the most optimistic face on her situation. "Don't blame yourself too much, Evelyn," he said shortly. "Even if you hadn't been there, this young man would have done the same thing for some other reason. There's a suicidal impulse just like there's a criminal one." Once again his voice faded. It was as if his innermost self were refusing to accept these words. Nonetheless, he continued, though it was plain he was fighting some kind of battle with himself. "These are the unknowns of the soul," he told her, groping for the right words. "Maybe they're attacks of mental illness—illness that's been inside the spirit for too long. But all of us should be afraid of suicide and crime. They're irrational acts; they can overtake anyone if the mind starts to lose itself, if its defenses are eaten away."

"Oh, Ernest, you're just trying to use that noble heart of yours to calm me down," said Evelyn, thoughtfully. "Maybe you haven't had a problem as devastating as this to trouble your conscience so far. Is that true?"

"Who? Me?" Ernest's voice stumbled. The question had disconcerted him. "Don't make me remember the past, Evelyn," he said abruptly. "For God's sake! I've done so many wrong things in my life already. I've seen so much treachery."

He stopped, realizing that he was now giving away too much. He forced a little embarrassed smile. His best maneuver at this point, he thought, was to go around the question rather than getting into its complexity. With maturity, one learns that kind of flexibility; it's a knack— the use of a mask to produce the appropriate psychological effect.

"You were telling me," he continued in a calmer

tone, "that the confessional didn't help you forget the young man who committed suicide? Your spiritual advisor wasn't able to calm that sensitive heart of yours?"

"I'll say it again, I always find a sort of moral vaccine against my smaller sins in confession. But in this case, I've never been able to find the peace I'm looking for. If only I hadn't hesitated so long between the two of them, I could have avoided this disaster completely. Now, all I have to do is think about poor Túlio and all the circumstances of his death come rushing back; and right away the guilt starts."

"Don't let it bother you so much," Ernest said. "You're too young for that. Of course, you're very sensitive right now. But that won't always be true. The self is like a hand that gets calluses, little by little, from working in the fields; the more suffering you see in life the more your sensitivity will be covered over. You'll develop a thick skin, as they say. Of course"—and all of a sudden the thoughtlessness of his response struck him— "if we do manage to get our health back, we'll see enough suicides, treachery, and disaster to last us for years."

It was now Evelyn's turn to sit in thought for a while. To Ernest she gave the impression of someone trying to heal inner wounds. Finally, she asked, determined to get some answers, "You've been studying the sciences of the soul. Do you truly and honestly believe we'll meet the people we love again—after we die, I mean?"

Ernest shrugged his shoulders—a gesture of complacency that belied his real feeling. "I don't know why," he said, "but that question makes me think of that old saying of Shakespeare's—'The wretched have no medicine other than hope.' Yes, I do have good reason to believe we'll see each other again. At the same time, I realize the conviction is based on my current situation—my organic state, let's say. Have you ever noticed, Evelyn, how ideas and words are usually the children of circumstances? Imagine, for instance, that we had our old health and strength back, and we were strong and looking good; then pretend that we were at some social function—a dance, for instance. Well, under those circumstances, this topic we have been talking about today would never occur to us. It would be totally inappropriate"

"That's true."

"But this dreadful disease now gives us the right to bring together new sources and new interpretations concerning life and death. And, as far as the conclusions we might come to, I have to believe that life doesn't stop at the grave. We ought to remember that old expression from the romantic novels: 'The romance ends, but life goes on.' Our bodies are like clothes that will fall off our backs one day. But our spirits will go on. Always."

"Do you ever think of someone special that you would like to find in the *after life*?"

He smiled enigmatically. "I can think of someone I would like *not* to find," he said in a joking manner.

"Well, I don't understand the humor. But it's a relief to hear you talk about the future with so much con-viction."

"You can't—and shouldn't—lose confidence in the future, Evelyn. Remember, above everything else, you're a Christian, the disciple of a Master who came back from the tomb on the third day."

Evelyn didn't smile this time. Instead she turned her gaze far beyond the rose-tinged clouds now reflecting the colors of the setting sun. Ernest's unexpected observations on the afterlife had deeply shaken her faith—the faith that she would survive exactly in the way her teachers had always insisted.

After a time, she looked back toward her new friend and prepared to say goodbye: "Well, Ernest," she said, "if there is another life beyond this one, and if it's God's will for us to undergo the *big change* soon, I believe we'll see each other again, and be friends too—over there."

"Why not?" he said merrily. "If I can foresee the end of this poor body of mine, I can certainly keep a firm, positive thought about our next meeting."

"So will I."

"When are you going back to São Paulo?"

"Tomorrow morning."

"Is there a date for the operation yet?"

"My husband and the doctor are deciding it. But I'll be facing it next week, I believe. How about you?"

"I'm not certain. Maybe in a few more days. I don't want to put it off too long. But will you tell me the name of your hospital?"

Evelyn thought for a while and said, "Ernest, we're

both suffering from a rare and insidious disease. Isn't that enough for us to get close to each other? Let's wait for the future and not worry about it. If we get through this crisis, I believe with all my heart that God will arrange a new meeting between us right here on Earth. If not, our friendship in *another world* will fall under the designs of Providence."

Ernest laughed at the forthrightness of this new profession. Then, walking slowly, the two of them walked back to the hotel together, silent for the most part and very much moved by this, their first and perhaps last encounter on Earth.

Chapter 4

RENOVATION

E velyn thought again of the comforting presence of Ernest, her little known friend, when her husband, Caio Serpa, left her in the large hospital room the day before her operation. Ensconced there now, she lay in bed, turning over strange thoughts in her mind. She was too young and too sure of her own recovery to seriously consider a bad outcome. But, as she lay alone, waiting for the nurse, Ernest's words kept coming back to her, setting her imagination on fire.

Yes, she was about to undergo a risky operation, she thought. She might never see her family again. And if she died, where would she go? When she was a little girl, she had believed explicitly in the existence of Heaven and Hell, the destiny of all human beings after death, according to the old Catholic dictates. Now, however, with science exploring even the cosmos, she was intelligent enough to realize how tactful her old confessor had been when he had spoken about the new perspectives that will influence certain points of religious doctrine. This learned and generous friend had taught her to maintain an unshakable faith in God, in the divine apostolate of Jesus Christ, and in the transcendent ministry of the saints. Yet she decided that, while accommodating these perspectives, she might as well put aside all the claims of human authority where the aspects and causes of Divine Providence were concerned.

Her train of thought changed for a time. The idea of death came to her more strongly than it had for a long while, but she rejected it. She wanted health, physical well-being; she longed for restoration, for life. And suddenly, in the midst of these thoughts, she paused and her mind went back to her problems at home. Obviously, she was going through some rough times in her marriage, she told herself, but she had reason to expect improvements in that area. She was still in the full bloom of her femininity, and lacked only her physical strength to make it perfect. As soon as she got well, she decided, she was going to try to remove the *other* woman from her husband's life and so transform her romantic relationship with him that he would have no other choice but to return her tender love, without the unkindness and arguments. Besides, she felt she had a great deal to do in the world. Yes, she *should* want life, and fight for it whatever the cost; and she *should* feel useful—not just to her relatives, but also to the less fortunate. No doubt, she could lessen poverty wherever she found it.

Thinking about the needy moved her. How many poor people lived all around her, separated from her only by walls? Why hadn't she ever thought of that before? She'd spent her entire existence as a satellite moving around three people: her husband, her mother, and her stepfather. It didn't seem enough now.

Yes, why shouldn't she regain her old strength, renew her life—live again? She was going to put all thoughts of death out of her mind and concentrate with all her strength on one thing—her recovery. She had read many books by psychologists and learned from them of how important a person's mental attitude can be in matters of health. So she aspired to recover. *I am going to get well—I am going to get well*; it would become an affirmation for her. She was going to repeat it as often as possible with all her emotional strength. And she would have other affirmations too, choosing only words loaded with energy that could better redefine her state of mind.

"And, yes," she thought to herself, "I should pray, too!"

As she formulated this idea, her eyes fell on a crucifix hanging on the wall across from her bed. She got up and walked over to it, contemplating the sublime face, which the artist had captured with great feeling. She crossed herself and spoke, more with her heart's voice than with her lips, "Lord, have mercy on me!"

She looked at the head crowned with thorns, at the arms nailed to the cross, and it occurred to her that Jesus appeared in people's memory in this way to remind them of how inevitable death was. The idea was a shock, coming so soon after her resolution not to think of death,

and it sent shivers through her. She didn't know anymore whether she had a choice between life or death.
Hiding her face in her hands, she knelt, humbly, in front
of the delicate sculpture, and cried her eyes out.

Someone tapped her delicately on the shoulder.
"Why are you crying, ma'am?"

It was one of the pre-op nurses who had come to
prepare her for the operation the next day.

Evelyn got up, dried her tears, and smiled: "I'm
sorry."

"Oh, no, I'm the one who's disturbing you, Mrs.
Serpa, "the young woman said. "Please forgive me for
interrupting your prayers, but we have to hurry. Oh,
by the way, your husband is waiting outside." Evelyn
took the cue and left the room, though she returned
directly.

Her husband sat outside, reading a newspaper.
"So," he joked, pretending everything was fine, "today
it's the beauty parlor, tomorrow the return to health."

Caio's voice communicated at once a sense of energy and great tenderness. As a young lawyer, he was
already experienced in public relations, and had charm-
ing, though studied manners. He was also an authentic
representative of the upper class, without the least bit
of untidiness about him. Yet it's fair to say that the young
lawyer was all tied up inside, always struggling to hide
the enigma that was his own soul. His outward appearance reflected little of his inner life. He wasn't, by any
means, a sincere personality. His academic veneer
couldn't entirely blot out the remnants of his animal

nature either, as is usually the case with those who revel in their human impulses. To spiritual eyes at that moment, he gave evidence of deep anxiety.

He spoke to Evelyn with warmth and fondness and, after the first few words, came close to her and kissed her hair. Evelyn couldn't hide her happiness at this seeming change in him, and they talked together pleasantly and affectionately for once. She repeated her belief that she would fully recover, and Caio related his news. Her mother and stepfather, now at their small farm in the south, were just waiting for good news about the operation so they could come to visit when it was convenient to do so. Probably they would not come right away—they didn't want to show undue alarm—but they wanted to reassure their daughter of how happy they were that she was finally getting the right treatment.

Caio had other news as well. He had been talking to other doctors, friends of theirs, and he had been discovering things about her adrenal gland condition himself. Better yet, in Evelyn's case, the surgeon was optimistic. The only thing lacking now, with God's blessing, was the successful operation.

Caio's expression "God's blessings" gladdened his wife. Is something new happening to this confirmed, thirty-year-old atheist, thought Evelyn. He seemed more attentive—different—and she, unsophisticated in these matters, didn't realize that he might be faking it, that his conversations and all the optimism were simply a false front. In fact, neither their family doctor nor the surgeon had promised anything beyond exploratory surgery; their hopes for a good prognosis were, they frankly told him, limited. Even the cardiologist had hesitated to recommend surgery, and finally agreed only because Evelyn was deteriorating so fast. She was certainly dying, so why stand in the way of an operation that had an outside chance of saving her? Caio knew very well about the doctor's concerns. But despite this knowledge, he manufactured positive arguments, lying piously when talking about the results of her tests, which in fact, had come back with dire warnings about the seriousness of her condition.

That night, the lawyer slept over at the hospital to be by his wife's side. The next morning he even helped the assistant nurse administer tranquilizers, precursors of the anesthesia. Indeed, he gave Evelyn all the love and care he would have shown to a child of whom he was the zealous father.

On the day following the operation, the surgeon asked for a meeting with him.

What he heard made him turn white.

Evelyn, in the surgeon's best estimate, had only a few days to live. Caio should, the surgeon advised, take all the precautions necessary to make those days as comfortable as possible. He summed up his impressions in one stark phrase: "She seems like a rose, invaded and completely eaten away by worms."

Caio tried, but after these words, he found himself incapable of listening to any more medical explanations, filled as they were with talk of neoplasms, secondary foci, metastases, and tumors that reappear after removal. He sat in the office like someone turned to stone. Tears streaked down his face in long lines. The surgeon tried to comfort him, treating him with the affection and tenderness he might have shown a brother. Caio thanked the man for his concern, then rushed back to his wife's bedside. He was the soul of patience with her. And yet dread filled him. In the next few days and nights, he became her brother, her father, her teacher, her friend.

Quickly he got in touch with his in-laws, Brigitte and Amancio Terra. Within the hour the two were making their way up from the southern part of the state of São Paulo, leaving their prosperous farm behind, intent only on consoling their daughter in these, her last days. They arrived devastated but, around her, selected their words carefully, holding back their tears and reflecting the last embers of optimism that still remained in them.

Evelyn, rocked in this cradle of family devotion and improving in her own mind, came back home. There she was pampered as she hadn't been in a long time. The attacks of suffocation continued as always. But in spite of them, her family and friends were filled with encouraging words about her condition, and she listened to them with total confidence in their knowledge. This will pass, they told her. Nobody can avoid the complications of an operation as delicate as the one she had undergone. She should have hope and pray with faith.

Two weeks passed in this way, divided between calm seas and variable winds. Then came six days of continuous well-being. She was extremely thin and tired

easily, but she left her bed for a sofa; she ate almost normally, talked calmly, and took communion through the
courtesy of a kindly priest who visited her at home. In
the evenings, she asked her stepfather to read something light and engaging to her.

Then during the afternoon of the fifth day of hope,
she made an unexpected request. Would Caio take her
out, as they used to when they were engaged?

"Morumbi[6] in the evening," asked her mother, quiz-
zically.

"Oh, I just want to see the city all lit up at night,"
Evelyn said, justifying herself, "and you can only see
that from a distance. And, anyway, I long to see a starry
sky."

Caio called the doctor, who agreed there was no
harm in the idea.

Immediately Caio took the car out of the garage,
anxious to satisfy his wife. He picked her up in his arms,
as if she were a little child, and put her in the front seat
next to him. Then they drove away alone, leaving her
parents behind.

Finding herself again in the crowded streets, Evelyn
was fascinated and delighted, as she was later with the
view from Morumbi and all its splendid natural surroundings.

They rode along, and as he listened to her talk, Caio

---

[6] *Translator's Note: A district of the city of São Paulo, famous for its beautiful
mountain scenery and its lover's lane.*

became all tenderness. It was like rediscovering his old, beloved fiancée whom he had adored so madly years before. He felt guilt too, remembering his unfaithfulness to her. He would love to have confessed to her, to have asked her forgiveness; but, he realized, it wasn't the right moment for such talk. He stopped the car awhile, admiring her in the moonlight. With each passing moment he found her more sublime. Her eyes sparkled beneath the moon, and her head, when she moved it, seemed encircled by light.

He took her then in his strong arms with the anxiety of someone who wanted to snatch up a treasure and defend it. In an uncontrollable flight of tenderness he kissed her, many times—kissed her until he felt the warm tears rolling down her cold cheeks . She was crying from happiness.

Freed at length from the arms she adored, she rested her head on his shoulder and left it there, admiring the sky over them as if it were a gigantic field of silver flowers.

She searched for her husband's right hand and held it awhile. Finally she asked, "Caio, do you believe we'll meet again after we die?"

Abruptly, he changed the subject, started the car, forbade her in affectionate terms to return to the subject of these "sad things," as he called them. They then began to make their way back home. On the way, she remembered the easy understanding she had had with Ernest Fantini, her new friend from the spa. She couldn't explain it to herself, but she longed for Ernest's presence right now; she had found him so sweet, his conversation so gratifying. She thirsted for spiritual conversation . She wanted to talk about eternal life, to listen to someone talk on the same subject—someone on the same wavelength as herself. Her husband was, to her mind, like a strange violin that, for some reason, couldn't be tuned to respond to her bow. These sublime emotions were dying in her heart—dying for lack of growth, of interaction with another soul. She could only listen to Caio, only bless him, only approve of him.

One more day of peace went by, and then Evelyn awoke in the middle of an attack. From anguish to anguish, gasp to gasp, she reached her last evening on Earth. Her husband and parents did all they could to keep her that last night, and she could see clearly the deep sadness in their faces. But her eyes—the physical ones—were so tired that at length she couldn't resist any more; she closed them.

The moment of her liberation came just as the stars were growing faint in the predawn light. Leaving this world, Evelyn opened her eyes one last time, and found herself watching the arrival of a new morning.

Chapter 5

MEETING AGAIN

She became aware that she was in a spacious room with two large windows through which she could see the sky. "My, that was the deepest sleep I've ever had," she thought, "but now I seem to be waking up from it." She tried to remember, to size up her situation, but her memory, usually so good, failed her.

Where did it come from, this sudden amnesia?

She concentrated very hard and finally, slowly, the memories began to filter back. First, an indescribable nightmare had overtaken her. "I must have fainted," she thought. Then she had felt herself moving through an exotic world of images. The images forced her back in time. She began remembering her past, reviewing—without knowing why or how—all the stages of her short existence, reconstructing them even to the point of seeing herself at age two on the day her father was brought back home, dead. It was like watching a movie in which she was aware of the most intimate details of her being, the innermost energies of her mind. In this last scene, for instance, she had again heard her mother's screams, and had seen, in front of her, the shocked neighbors, though she had no idea of the tragedy that had befallen her. After that, the impression of a tremendous shock had swept over her, and something opened up in her brain. She saw herself above her own sleeping body—floating in mid-air. Finally, she had fallen into an irresistible sleep, and knew—nothing.

How long had she been in this strange stupor? Was she coming back to herself after collapsing from some special treatment? Why wasn't there one single relative beside her, helping her find answers to these questions.

She tried to get up, and did so easily. She inspected her surroundings and saw that she was no longer in her room at home. She must, she decided, have had one of her blackouts and been taken to a hospital. This large room, painted a restful light green, could only be her hospital room. On a nearby table sat a vase of sweet-smelling roses. Next to it, thin drapes danced slowly to the rhythm of a soft breeze. The breeze came through a set of odd-looking Venetian blinds, made of a substance that looked like crystal covered by an emerald-like lacquer. Everything was tasteful, simple, well thought out, comfortable and light.

Evelyn yawned, and stretched her arms. To her surprise, this movement didn't produce a single ache or pain. "Finally, finally," she thought happily, "I'm well!" The feeling of health infused her. She could attest to it: no suffering, no irritation. Indeed, she felt one thing that

wasn't entirely agreeable, but that too was a sign of returned strength; she wanted something to eat.

Where, she wondered, were her husband and parents? She wanted to yell out her happiness to them, tell
them she was cured. Everything she had gone through,
she wanted to say, hadn't simply been a waste. She spoke
a silent prayer, thanking God for giving her back her
health. Now she was anxious to thank her loved ones
as well.

Her heart was drunk with happiness and, unable
to calm it or herself, she looked for a service buzzer and
found one near her bed. She pressed the button, and
shortly a woman with an attractive-looking face came
in and bid her (very tenderly, very generously, Evelyn
thought) welcome. She returned this greeting as best
she could, then said, "Nurse, would you please call my
husband?"

"My instructions are to call the doctor before anyone else, and let him know you've come to."

"Very well," Evelyn agreed, "but I really do want
to contact my relatives and let them know how happy I
am."

"I understand," the other replied gently.

"Oh, I need to talk with someone!" Evelyn added
in her new, lively way, "What's your name?"

"Sister Lisa."

"Well, you probably know me. I am Evelyn Serpa.
Are my medical records here?"

"Yes."

"Sister Lisa, what in the world happened to me? I

feel all right, but I'm in such a strange mood. I can't describe it. "

"You have undergone a long surgery, that's all. Now you have to rest, recuperate."

Evelyn wasn't exactly surprised at these words, although she did think that the way in which they were spoken was odd—though why she couldn't say. She knew that she had been operated on, that she had gone through the painful removal of a tumor and gone home, where she had improved so much that she and her husband had taken a jaunt in his car to Morumbi. Nonetheless, here she was back in the hospital again, and she couldn't figure out why.

A number of questions formed in her mind. Distracted by them, she failed to notice the nurse press a small gray button on one of the walls. This was, in fact, a call to the doctor on duty who, dressed in white and looking very relaxed, came into the room in a couple of minutes, said hello to his patient, examined her, and smiled as if satisfied with what he found.

"Doctor . . . " Evelyn started—she was anxious to find out about her condition. She then asked for medical details, and how and when she would be able to see her husband and parents. It was only fair, wasn't it, to let her family know the good news about the success of her treatment?

The doctor listened to her patiently, and asked for her understanding. She would be returning to her relatives, he said, but first she needed some time to readjust. His hands rested lightly on her shoulders, as if he were calming his own daughter. "You're better, Evelyn," he explained, "much better, to tell the truth. But we still need to keep a close watch on your mental state. If you were to go near anyone or anything that caused you to remember your illness, you could suffer a setback. All your symptoms would return. Think about it. It really isn't to your benefit to rejoin your relatives just now."

Then with a look even more understanding, he added, "Try and cooperate."

Evelyn heard this pronouncement with tear-filled eyes, but accepted it with resignation. After all, she thought to herself, she should be grateful to these people. They had turned her new situation into such a blessing. It wouldn't be right to interfere with their procedures, which she couldn't really understand anyway.

She saw that the doctor was about to leave, and timidly asked if it was possible for her to read, and if it was, whether the hospital would lend her a book about the teachings of Jesus.

Curiously, she thought, the doctor seemed deeply moved by this request; he suggested the New Testament. Accordingly, within a few moments of his departure, the nurse came back with a copy of the Bible.

Alone again, Evelyn started to read the Sermon on the Mount, but the doctor's warning kept running through her mind. If she was cured—and she felt very much that she was—why should simple memories bring back her physical symptoms? She had been freed from those symptoms, and was aware at the moment of being caught up in an indescribable euphoria. A delicious

sensation of lightness had taken hold of her—her entire disposition had changed and she felt happier than
she had been in her whole life. Could these signs of her
physical health actually be so easy to lose?

She put down the book and immersed herself in a
new train of thought. What if she intensely visualized
the presence of Caio and her parents? Or focused on
the pain she had left behind? In short order, she tried
these exercises only to find herself, after a few minutes,
undergoing an attack. Quickly it engulfed her body. Her
extremities became cold and numb, while on the inside
she felt burning hot. Breathing suddenly became difficult, and her chest hurt as she tried to suck in air. Now
she tried to rid herself of these symptoms by concen-
trating on health, but it was too late. An intense pain
overcame her, and soon she was writhing in the torment
she had been so sure, a few moments earlier, she had
overcome .

Frightened, she pressed the buzzer and shortly the
nurse came hurrying to her aid. The doctor too reap-
peared and administered some sedatives. Neither he nor
the nurse reproached her, but in their eyes she read the
conviction that they understood everything. Without a
word, they let her know how aware they were of her
stubbornness; that they knew, most certainly, that she
hadn't paid attention to their warnings and had experi-
mented on herself, using some sort of visualization inappropriate to someone in her state. All the time, however, the doctor treated her with kindness, even as he
acted with the efficiency and energy of a professional.

He gave her something akin to an injection, pushing the pointed tip directly into her head, and then gave the nurse strict instructions about special procedures for putting her to sleep. It was advisable that she rest for a longer period of time, he said, and that her sleep be controlled by anesthetics. The patient could not and should not try to fix her ideas if she didn't want to suffer unnecessarily.

Evelyn heard all this through an increasing drowsiness. A few minutes later, she fell into a deep sleep. When she awoke, many hours later, she was newly conscious of the need to take better care of herself or risk the occurrence of another panic attack.

She now felt very hungry and, expressing this to one of the nurse's aides, she was soon served with a hot and nourishing broth that, from the delicious taste of it, might have been manna from heaven. She kept a close watch on her thoughts and moods, and began recuperating well. She realized she was undergoing a special type of treatment, the power and effectiveness of which she could not underestimate.

A week of absolute rest followed, during which her only entertainment was books chosen by the staff. At the end of the week she began getting up, walking around her room, exercising a little. She noted a definite difference in herself. Her feet seemed lighter, as if she had lost weight, and ideas came into her mind in a downpour, strong and beautiful, almost taking form before her eyes.

One afternoon, feeling more inclined than usual to

resume her normal movement, she walked over to one of the windows, which faced an enormous patio. She was staying on the third floor of the hospital. Below her sauntered dozens of persons, talking happily together. Many were seated around a water fountain that had been built in the midst of a large, flower-laden garden.

This serene picture attracted her. She was anxious for company, having spent some time now under the austere regimen demanded by her treatment. In view of that, she asked one of the nurse's aides, could she go down and meet someone? After all, she suggested optimistically, a nursing home is rather like a cruise ship, where the people on board naturally meet and become interested in each other. The aide smiled at the comparison and, lending an arm for support, helped her patient down into the garden.

Yes, Evelyn thought, she could entertain herself very well down here. The surroundings would do her good, and at the same time she would be able to make a friend or two.

Left alone she began to notice the faces of the people around her. It seemed to her that she was in the middle of a large family whose members shared similar interests even if they were almost totally unknown to each other—very like, she thought, people at a health spa. All had signs, too, of being convalescents, and one could easily guess, from their appearance, what sicknesses they were recovering from.

Evelyn was wondering about how best to strike up a conversation with someone when she saw a man, seated not far away, who was staring at her in obvious amazement.

Oh! Wasn't that gentleman Ernest Fantini, the friend she had made so unexpectedly at the mineral spring resort?

Her heart beat a little faster. She raised her arm and waved toward him, assuring him he would be more than welcome to join her.

He got up from the armchair in which he was seated and came toward her at a quickening pace. It was Ernest indeed. " Evelyn! Evelyn," he said excitedly. "Is it really you I'm seeing here?"

"It's me all right!" she answered, and her happiness was so great at finding him that she couldn't help crying.

The newcomer was no stranger to emotion on that unforgettable occasion himself. Tears also rolled down his stern and handsome face—tears he was trying, even as he smiled, to sweep away, and which frankly embarrassed him a little.

Chapter 6

EMPATHY

"How long have you been here?"
"I really don't know, " answered Ernest, eager to pursue the conversation. "But I've been thinking a lot about our encounter at Poços de Caldas,"[7] he added, "I've always hoped I'd see you again."

"That's so nice of you!"

Evelyn told him then about the puzzling events she had been experiencing—how she had awakened in this hospital, one completely unknown to her, having obviously been transferred here from home by her family. The only thing she remembered clearly was passing out after one of the worst attacks she had ever gone through. And she added, smiling at the idea, she had had the distinct impression, during the attack, that she was *dying*.

---

[7] *Translator's Note: Poços de Caldas – The location of their first encounter. A city in the state of Minas Gerais famous for its mineral spring resorts and health spas.*

How long she had been unconscious she didn't know. She only remembered waking up out of a deep, dreamless sleep, to find herself here in a room on the third floor. Since then she had been trying to penetrate the cloud of mystery the management of the place had, for some reason, thrown up around her; they had, for instance, refused to let her call her husband.

Ernest listened attentively, but said nothing. Around them sat various people who chatted casually or read, or simply walked about the garden. The air was heavy with the scent of roses, myosotis, jasmines, sweet williams, begonias, and other flowers, all growing under what resembled almond, fig, and magnolia trees.

At the end of Evelyn's remarks, which he listened to with considerable curiosity, Ernest, with an unusual brightness in his eyes, confirmed his friend's account. He had felt as if he were surrounded by hot coals, he said, and he had experienced the same strange feeling of withdrawal from his physical self that she had. All this had happened right after his surgery, just as he was returning to his room, or so he thought. He had also undergone the same extraordinary phenomena of memory and retrospection that Evelyn had just mentioned. He saw himself suddenly drawn back into the past, revisiting it even as far back as his early infancy. Afterwards, he slept heavily. Then, ten days ago, he woke up in this hospital without a clue as to how long he'd been unconscious. He too was puzzled over the protocol of the place, since he hadn't been allowed to make the slightest contact with his wife or daughter, to whom he had said goodbye in the hospital room a few hours before his operation. All of this was, to say the least, making him uneasy.

Evelyn, he noted, had experienced her baffling fainting spell at home, near her loved ones. He, on the other hand, had left his family while he was in the throes of intense anxiety; and now, communicating with them seemed to be impossible. This hospital wasn't, in any case, the same one he had gone to for his surgery. To tell the truth, he was starting to doubt that he was even in the state of São Paulo: The sky seemed somehow different at night and the swimming pool he used was filled with the purest water imaginable. It was possible, however, that the hospital used a special filter to treat water from the city reservoir.

Ernest asked, "And how about you? Have you been to the hot springs here yet?"

"Not yet," Evelyn answered.

"You'll see why I find this place so very unusual when you do go there."

"Are you so sure I'll go?" replied Evelyn. She gave him a roguish look and appeared a bit more resigned to her situation.

"Yes, indeed. I've heard that hydrotherapy is compulsory around here." He smiled in a significant way as he spoke these words, and then declared, anxiety coloring his every word, "You know what might be a more reasonable hypothesis? I believe we're in a psychiatric hospital; our relatives have had us committed. I don't know anything about medicine, but our adrenal problems must be affecting our minds. Maybe we've become unbalanced, mentally out of touch. Maybe complete isolation was medically necessary."

"Why do you think so?" Evelyn was very pale.

" Mrs. Serpa—."

"Please, Ernest, stop calling me 'Mrs.' she interrupted. "We're friends now; more like brother and sister. I insist on it."

"Very well then, Evelyn" agreed Ernest. Then he continued, "For instance, you should see these funny gadgets they use—this is right before the medicinal baths. They hook us up to these gadgets to apply some kind of radiation to our heads, I think. And believe me, they work; all the patients show signs of gradual improvement. I went for a total immersion for the first time the day before yesterday, and ever since then I've felt more lucid and lighter—always lighter."

"Haven't you been in a better frame of mind generally since you woke up?"

"Not really. Every time I start to worry about not hearing from my wife and daughter, these violent attacks come on. All I have to do is think of them, or my surgery, and I start to suffocate. It gets so bad, I almost faint."

Evelyn remembered her own experience, but said nothing. She was feeling more uneasy than ever.

"The people in charge here answer my questions very guardedly, and I believe they're trying hard to keep us all in a tranquil state—to keep us feeling agreeable. I think it's possible that we might have gone through some psychic trauma and that we're now in the process of recovering our mental equilibrium, little by little. The therapy we're undergoing, it seems to me, is completely mental in nature. Just yesterday, I made my old complaint and asked to speak with my people. Do you know what the nurse on duty told me, just as self-assured as can be?"

"No, what?"

"'Brother Fantini, calm yourself. Your relatives know all about your absence.' 'But don't they want to talk to me? Don't they even phone me?' I asked. And she said, 'Your wife and daughter know they can't expect you back home so soon.' Really, it was more than I could take. I continued to insist. I demanded that something be done immediately to remedy the situation, but she only said, 'That's all I can tell you for now.' "

"And what do you think it all means?"

"Well, for lack of a better explanation, that we have been, without our knowing it, under some form of mental delusion," Ernest suggested. He sounded almost happy again. "And that most likely we're now coming out of our psychological darkness and into a normal state of consciousness. The doctors and nurses are trying to keep us from any sort of preoccupation with life on the outside; and they're absolutely right. We're still subject to a slight trace of mental imbalance at the moment, I think, and it could do a great deal of damage to our emotions and ideas to push it too far—like the small distortions that affect electromagnetic waves, breaking their symmetry."

"That's possible, I imagine," Evelyn said.

An expressive pause followed these words. Ernest seemed to lose himself in his own inner world; it was he, nonetheless, who finally broke the silence. "Evelyn," he said, "when you had that terrible attack you just mentioned, had you made your confession? What did the priest tell you? Did he give you any pointers?"

There was anguish behind these questions that very much surprised and confused Evelyn, but she fired back, "Why do you want to know, Ernest? Yes, I did make my confession before my fainting spell—as often as I could. But why ask now? Are you making fun of me?"

Ernest wasn't kidding, though. His eyes revealed an undeniable anxiety.

"Oh, don't worry about it. I was just asking," he said, and tapped the fingers of his left hand on the tripod in front of him. "In a precarious situation, like the one we're in, we need all the help we can get. I just remembered that you have a religion and that I'm still a man without faith."

Ernest had barely gotten out this last sentence when a young girl, walking with two friends a short distance away from them, collapsed in a sudden fit of hysteria.

"No!—I don't wanna be here no more!" she yelled. "I wanna go home... my own house! Mommy!—where's my mommy? Open the door, you mean people! Please, won't anybody help me get over the wall? Police! Call the police!"

It was, without doubt, a mental breakdown, but there was so much suffering in that voice that the people around the girl got up and turned toward her, astonished. In another instant, a woman wearing the nursing insignia of the hospital appeared. Soon she had opened up a path through the growing group of onlookers. She bent down and, radiating patience and kindness, took the out-of-control young girl in her arms as if she had been her mother. She lifted the girl up, and without a hint of disapproval in her voice, began consoling her. "Daughter, who told you that you wouldn't go back home? That you wouldn't see your mother again?" Her voice was all warmth and tenderness. "Our doors are always open. Please, come with me."

"Oh, sister, I'm sorry...I'm sorry!" The young girl, suddenly calmed by the strong, kind arms around her, sighed. "I know it's not right to complain so much," she said, "but I miss Mommy and my house so much! I've been here forever, and nobody's come to see me. Nobody. I know I'm sick I'm getting all healed here. But I haven't heard from anyone!"

The nurse listened to her calmly, and only promised, "You will see them." Then, putting her arms around the girl's shoulders, she added, "But for now, you need rest!"

The girl, who saw in the caring nurse the maternal warmth she so desperately needed at the moment, lay her blonde head on the woman's chest and walked away with her, sobbing. Evelyn and Ernest, who had approached the spot hoping to offer help, watched the scene half-grieved and half-disappointed. They thirsted for some explanation. What were they to conclude from this sick girl's teary-eyed plea, troubled as she was by homesickness? What kind of hospital was this? An asylum? A recuperation center for patients with amnesia?

Evelyn's curiosity had now gotten the better of her. Impulsively, she came up to a sympathetic-looking woman who had been watching the scene closely and whose white hair reminded her of her mother's. As discretely as she could, she said to her, "Excuse me, ma'am. You don't know me, but our ailments here make us family, in a way. Can you tell us anything about that poor girl?"

"Who me? Me? Daughter, I don't know anything about the life of anyone around here," answered the lady.

"But listen, please. Do you know where we are? In what hospital?"

The white-haired matriarch drew closer to Evelyn who, with this movement, took a step backwards toward Ernest. "Don't you know?" The woman whispered. To Evelyn's undisguised surprise, she next turned her piercing eyes to Ernest. "And how about you?" she said to him.

"We don't know anything," said Ernest, politely.

"Well, someone told me that we're all dead here, that we don't live on Earth any more."

At this news, Ernest took out a handkerchief and began to wipe the sweat that had started to pour from his forehead. Evelyn staggered, almost fainted. The unknown lady stretched out a hand to steady her and, looking worried, said "Daughter, calm down. The regimen is very strict here. If you show any sign of weakness or being out of control, I don't know when they'll let you come back to the patio."

"Let's rest," suggested Ernest. He gave his arm to Evelyn, and with the helpful lady supporting her on the other side, the three of them made their way to a large bench, placed under a nearby fig tree, and sat down to gather their thoughts.

Chapter 7

ALZIRA BREAKS THE NEWS

"Let's talk," said their new friend invitingly. She was, however, wary of the hospital's security services, especially the possibility that someone might have noticed Evelyn's shock at the news she had given them. She advised them to avoid attracting attention to themselves.

Ernest understood her point and tried to help. He pretended to ignore the paleness that had come over Evelyn, and to make the necessary introductions with apparent calm.

"My name is Alzira Campos," said the older woman, "and I live in São Paulo." She gave her address, described her family and neighborhood, and then added, "I fell down at home, and they brought me here to the hospital unconscious. Since then, by my own reckoning, I've been waiting to be released for the past two months." While this exchange was going on between the two, Evelyn slowly regained her composure.

Ernest asked, "Do you feel as if your health is back to normal?"

"Completely."

"Do you know anyone in authority here who could tell you how long exactly you can expect to stay?"

"Yes. Sister Letitia—she helped me at first in the medicinal baths. She told me day before yesterday that I'll shortly be able to decide whether I should remain here or not."

"What did she mean by '*whether you should remain here or not?*'"

"Well, she certainly knows how much I want to go back home, and she must have seen that, for me, getting *that* kind of assurance was particularly annoying."

"Did you ask her anything else?"

"Yes. I begged her for a clearer picture of things, more details. She only told me, very politely, as they do here, 'You'll understand better, later.' "

" Alzira," Ernest whispered, but with a note of firmness, "you don't think we're in a mental institution, a madhouse, do you?"

The older woman looked around her, as if she were afraid of being watched by threatening guards. "If we're going to talk about something this serious," she said, "we shouldn't leave out our friend here. She can get something to bring her around, you know. Let's order a tonic—that will help her out." With these words, she pressed a small button on top of the table in front of them. Soon a young aide appeared, wanting to know how he could be of service. Alzira ordered refreshments for three.

"What flavor?"

"Apple."

In a moment the aide was back with three glasses filled with a pink and lightly scented liquid, sitting on a tray the color of sapphire.

"This is the best refreshment I've found so far here. It acts as a mild tonic," said the woman when they were by themselves again. Evelyn took a sip, and then drank avidly—having tasted, she thought, a nectar that felt almost vapor-like going down. The drink acted as a powerful restorative and brought back her vitality and mental balance in short order. "I'm better, thank God!" she said suddenly. Alzira smiled, ready to talk now and describe for her new friends everything she knew about their situation.

"Going back to what we were saying," Ernest whispered, "don't you think that we're getting some sort of specialized treatment, from a mental point of view?"

"I thought so at first," Alzira explained. "Notice that here our thoughts are always lighter, our minds are always clearer. Ideas flow so much faster and more spontaneously, until they seem to form shapes on their own. I agree that we're living in a different type of psychological atmosphere, very different from the one we were used to before coming here. But, despite this, I don't believe we're in a madhouse. You know, we're surrounded by a very active city, with residences, schools, institutions, temples, industries, vehicles, public entertainment."

"What?" Evelyn and Ernest spoke together.

"This is a relatively large city, I tell you. No less than a hundred thousand inhabitants, they say, and with a superbly efficient administration."

"Have you had any experience of the outside? Have you been beyond these walls?" Ernest was dying of curiosity.

"Sure, last week I got permission to visit a family. I didn't know them—just went along with a couple of friends of mine. It was the first time I had left the hospital up to then. And I can assure you it was a really nice outing, despite the shock I got at the end of it."

Ernest asked, "What did you see? Who did you see?"

"O don't worry! You'll find out everything in your own proper time. The city is beautiful. It's in a kind of valley and filled with the most unusual buildings, architecturally speaking. All of them seem to be carved out of jade and crystal and lapis lazuli. And it has lovely parks covered with gardens. Walking the streets is a fascinating experience. Nicomedes, whose house we visited, was so polite when he invited us in. He introduced us to a beautiful young woman, his daughter Coreen, and I took to her immediately. She's very close to one of my friends, who wanted to talk to her about some kind of work. Coreen also mentioned how happy everyone in the house was because of some expected arrival, and then she showed us the new chandeliers, the paintings, and some splendid vases.

"Everything was a crescendo of sweet surprises for

me. Then the bombshell!. We were on the terrace, admiring a hanging jasmine garden, when we heard Lizst's *Dream of Love* being played on a piano. Her father, Coreen told us, was a master pianist. The music was so sweet I asked if we could go inside to listen to it. Our hostess obliged and took us immediately into the living room. It was fascinating. Nicomedes was absorbed. He looked as if he was in a world of deep happiness, which radiated out from his inner self in the form of melodies—remarkable melodies that followed one after the other. At one point I said, 'He seems to be in an extended ecstasy, he plays as if he's praying.' 'Oh, yes, we're very happy indeed,' replied his daughter, 'since my mother is coming this week.' I asked, 'Has she been traveling?' 'She's coming from Earth,' the girl answered, her voice utterly guileless.

"I might have been stabbed through the heart, the shock was so terrible. I felt suffocated, and, ill prepared as I was for this news, I had a painful attack. This simple idea—that we were in a place outside of the world I always knew—brought back all the symptoms of my angina, something I hadn't experienced in a long time. Coreen understood my situation, and without saying a word, brought me a sedative.

"My state of mind, I noticed, had an effect on everyone in the room, and Nicomedes stopped his playing suddenly in the middle of a beautiful nocturne. I was about to faint. The group gathered around and took me outside for some fresh air. They put me in an armchair made of stone— some kind of marble, I thought—

and only after I had grasped the back of it and felt with my hands how rigid and hard it was, did I start to get my composure back. After a while I looked up at the sky, and saw the full moon, shining brightly and beautifully, and with that sight my peace of mind returned. The scare I had had was unfounded, I realized, and then I thought, Why shouldn't a city, a village, a hamlet, named *Earth* exist somewhere? The scene around me was absolutely a part of the world and no doubt Nicomedes' wife was coming from an unknown village.

"I was still turning these ideas over in my mind when Nicomedes asked, 'How long has Sister Alzira been with us?' 'A little over two months,' answered one of my friends. And that was that. Nothing else was said about me, but the visit ended then and there. Back at the hospital, my friends, two excellent nurses by the way, didn't say one word about the fright I had had."

"Have you talked to anybody else about this?" The curious Ernest asked.

"Well, during the baths, I sometimes listen to this one and that one. They're all a little unsure about it, but most of them suspect we're in another life."

"They can't say that with absolute certainty, though," interjected Evelyn.

"Only Mrs. Tambourini. She's fully convinced that we're no longer on Earth. She told me she has been going to a magnetic-healing study group, right here at the hospital, and undergoing some tests that have convinced her she's no longer in a physical body. I listened to her closely, and she even invited me to participate in some of the experiments. I said no, though. These *stories of clairvoyance and reincarnation* don't go down very well with people of my faith."

"Ah, you're a Catholic," Evelyn said, "like me?"

"Oh, yes!"

"Since we're in a large city, do we have priests here?"

"Yes, we do."

"Have you spoken to any of them?"

"No, but I was invited to visit a church and plan on going, as soon as I'm allowed. But I have to tell you— I've heard from good sources that the priests in these parts are very different. "

"In what way?"

"They say these priests are doctors, professors, scientists, and workers. And that they don't restrict themselves to faith work. They do give spiritual help in the name of Jesus, however, and are very efficient and positive."

By this time, Ernest noticed that the patio was emptying, and all the patients going back inside. Alzira, too, said goodbye shortly but promised to meet them again at another time. Soon afterwards, Ernest and Evelyn went back to their own rooms, but not before agreeing to see each other the following day.

Chapter 8

CULTURAL MEETING

E rnest and Evelyn enjoyed many hours of friendly conversation there on the patio—hours during which they held absorbing conversations and tried, as friends do, to comfort each other. More than fifteen days had passed since their first meeting at the hospital, and Evelyn had become as familiar with the therapeutic baths as her friend. Both of them had also gotten in contact with Mrs.Tambourini, the person Alzira had suggested as her most knowledgeable acquaintance. This helpful person had promised to take them, as soon as she possibly could, to the Sciences of the Spirit Institute, which operated right there, near the large garden.

Mrs. Tambourini's explanations of their circumstances, they agreed, were the most enlightening they had heard so far. The three met almost daily, with Mrs. Tambourini guiding them toward an increasingly deeper analysis of their situation, and toward a wider examination of their mental perceptions. These two subjects alternated according to their relative importance at the moment. At times, Mrs. Tambourini would request that they study the extreme sense of lightness they were now experiencing, or the agility of the subtle bodies they now had, or the unique way they could express their thoughts, as if the ideas sprouted from their brains in the form of images, far exceeding their normal recall abilities. They were to investigate, too, the new life they found themselves in, and the incidents of telepathy that were so much more common over here. Despite the continued use of spoken language, it took only a higher level of affinity between persons, it seemed, for them to be able to understand each other perfectly in complicated affairs and without the use of words.

They listened to all these reasoned opinions and were pleased—except in one matter. Mrs. Tambourini completely accepted the notion that they were disembodied beings living in some division of the Spirit World.

Well, they had come to have a great deal of respect for her, but this was one notion they had trouble accepting.

One day Evelyn was sitting on the grass, near Ernest's feet. He was perched on a small footstool, and began their usual conversation with a worried analysis. "It's true—every day I feel lighter, always lighter," he said, "and as a result, I'm losing control of myself. The feelings just rush up from my heart straight to my head—it's like underground water rising up to gush out of a fountain. And once they're there, the emotions turn into thoughts that are automatically translated into words. I don't seem to be able to stop them any more."

"I agree," Evelyn replied. 'That defines my own state of mind exactly. But, listen, Ernest," she said, touching the trunk of a large tree beside her, "what do you see here?"

"A tree trunk."

"And over there, in that flower bed?"

"Carnations."

"All right, then, everywhere we look, matter and nature are exactly the same as we have always known them. Ask yourself—if that's so, could this really be the Spirit World?"

"I agree—it seems crazy, absurd. Maybe we just haven't studied our situation in enough depth yet, but—"

"But!"

"Well, we can't start jumping to conclusions."

"You're just being influenced by Mrs. Tambourini's ideas. Admit it."

"Not really. I arrive at my own conclusions."

"How about this, then. If we're dead for the ones *we* love, why haven't the loved ones of our families, the ones who were in this new life before us, come to see us yet? Our grandparents, for example, and our close friends that we saw dying?"

"And who told you they haven't?"

"How do you figure they have?"

"Like this, Evelyn. Try and remember basic lessons from home—mine or yours or anyone's. A television set captures images we don't see, but it reproduces them with absolute fidelity on the screen. A portable radio picks up music and messages we don't hear—but all the same, it plays them for us with perfect clarity. It's very likely that we're being seen and heard—we just don't have the necessary equipment to listen and watch on this plane yet."

"How about prayers, Ernest? If we're spirits, free from our material bodies, somebody on Earth must have remembered us in their prayers—your wife, your daughter, my parents, my husband."

"I can't say. We don't know much about the mechanisms of spirit relations, and let's face it, we aren't very well educated in the science of the soul. Maybe we're being sustained here by the power of prayer—the prayers of the ones we love or the ones who still love us."

"What do you mean, sustained?"

"Well, has either of us ever received a bill from this hospital? Who do we owe for all the care and kindness we're getting here? We're not buying the new clothes or accessories we use. Have either of us asked a nurse the famous question, 'Who pays?'"

"Yes, I asked. "

"And what was the answer?"

"'Your loved ones.'"

"And who are they, as you see it?"

"My husband and my parents, in my case."

"Maybe so, but I have my doubts. At first I thought we were recuperating in a mental hospital. But with every passing day we reach a higher level of consciousness where our thinking is concerned. Now, if we had both had nervous breakdowns and were in a madhouse, our recovery wouldn't be so fast. Don't you agree?"

At this point, this interesting conversation was interrupted.

Mrs. Tambourini came rushing toward them.

A meeting on spiritual culture had been arranged for that very night, she told them, and since it was about to start they would have to hurry to make it.

So it was that, after getting the necessary permission from the hospital staff, they found themselves at the meeting at around seven o'clock that evening. With them was their friend Mrs. Tambourini, who introduced them to the instructor on duty, Brother Claude.

In the classroom sat twenty-three people waiting for the study session to start. These students welcomed them, and immediately they felt at home. In one corner of the room, they noticed, was an enormous globe, apparently for use in the lecture that evening.

The instructor began the meeting by explaining that the class would be conducted in the form of a discussion. Its members should look on him as just another friend—someone who had his own personal biases but was interested in the lessons of wisdom, someone who had some objective answers and at times ambiguous ones, but was always willing to explore new hypotheses.

"What is today's topic, if you please?" asked an elegant lady.

"Existence on Earth."

With this announcement, the leader of the group

began his lecture. During the course of it, he offered invaluable teachings concerning the function of Earth in the cosmic economy.

At the end he said, "Think about it, friends. Can any of us, with such a partial understanding of the nature of reality, claim to be wise enough to make statements about that reality based only on our personal impressions? We can't ignore the fact that Earth is a huge machine in space, carrying almost three billion people[8] as it makes its way through the Universe—although none of us knows exactly how or by what force. All we know is that this colossal globe goes around the Sun, in an elliptic orbit, at a speed of 67,000 miles per hour. We also know that while some people are standing on the topmost part of the globe, others are standing on its bottom-most part and upside down in relation to the first group—although neither is aware of the fact. Furthermore, not too long ago most people would have said that matter in a landscape consists of solid elements at rest; today, any elementary school student knows that this idea is imaginary; instead, all matter is formed of a mixture of electrons, protons, and neutrons enveloped in energy and light. We can also say that human beings live in borrowed bodies, breathing and responding, without much effort on their part, to the demands nutrition makes on them. How can we, then, relying only on our limited physical senses, ever say anything final

---

[8] Translator's Note: Probably correct for the time this book was written, 1968. Closer to six billion in 2000.

about the causes, processes, trials, and ultimate goal of our earthly existence?"

Here the lecturer paused, and a gentleman began to ask, "From these deductions, do you mean to say—"

"That life on Earth has to be interpreted as a special work for the spirit," interjected the lecturer, already aware of what the man was going to say. "Each of us is born to perform a special task. It's possible that in performing it we'll evolve and go on to other tasks, always more important. Because of this, it isn't possible to rob human beings of their religious principles without doing great damage to them. Science will always advance, always go on discovering the secrets of the Universe, solving problems, stirring up new challenges to the human capacity for investigation. But it is faith that will sustain humanity in its accomplishments and the trials it will be called on to go through. The spirit is reborn in the physical world as many times as necessary to improve itself, better itself, enlighten itself. To the extent that it improves, it becomes more and more aware that existence in the body is an obligation, a mission to be fulfilled, and that an account will be called for at the end of the job."

Throughout his explanations, the lecturer showed such a wealth of knowledge that interruptions were few. Without straying from the main point of the lecture—in which he was no doubt trying to prepare his listeners to accept their new spiritual state calmly—he remarked, "If God's laws reveal themselves so clearly and richly in every sphere of physical experience, would God by some chance neglect us when we cross the frontier of death? We talk, frightened, about the slaughter of human life during wartime. On the other hand, what can we conclude about human lives being methodically extinguished during times of peace? Would God be indifferent to our destinies anywhere in the Universe? Would God, Who inspires the graduation of nourishment in both child and adult, abandon an individual after his passage, when that very person lives and functions in a sphere of action in which predictability and order exalt the grandeur of life?"

These last points were so enigmatic that no one there quite grasped their significance. In fact, most of the attendees weren't aware that, through talks like these, they were subtly being prepared to admit their spiritual reality without the admission being a shock to them.

Now a pause occurred while the instructor examined certain geographic positions on the giant globe. Evelyn found the courage to ask: "Brother Claude, does everyone experience the same sensations after death?"

"No, not at all," came the answer. "Each of us is a world unto him or herself. Each individual, then, after leaving the earthly vehicle, will find emotions, places, people, affections, opportunities that accord with the performance of certain obligations or—to put it another way—to the duties he or she has been assigned during earthly existence. Nobody will have knowledge that he or she did not work hard to master, and nobody will show qualities that haven't been acquired."

Claude continued to lecture in this way, making points full of beauty and logic. At the end of his explanations, which they pronounced brilliant, Ernest and Evelyn felt comforted and happy—like voyagers thirsty for values of the soul, who this evening had drunk from a fountain of spiritual light.

Chapter 9

BROTHER CLAUDE

After class, Ernest and Evelyn lingered behind. They might as well take advantage of Mrs. Tambourini's recommendation and talk with Brother Claude, who was happy to meet with them. During the course of the conversation, Brother Claude explained that he didn't live at the Institute, but most certainly they should come to his own place one day for a bit of chat. He and his wife would be glad to welcome them. Furthermore, seeing as how Mrs. Tambourini herself had recommended him as someone capable of assisting them with important questions, he was at their disposal. He would help in whatever way he could, though frankly he didn't feel that he at all merited the trust Mrs. Tambourini had placed in him.

After a while, the trio went out into the moonlit garden of the Institute, and joined one of a number of small student groups lounging casually there. The three sat together at a table, and talked excitedly. It was extraordinary how familiar everything seemed; there was nothing here that didn't suggest an earthly setting. Because of that, and despite Ernest's preoccupied expression—he looked so uncertain, so anxious—Evelyn was feeling self-assured, absolutely convinced that she was in an authentic corner of her own familiar world.

"I understand that you would like to find out more about your new life here," said Brother Claude, "Mrs. Tambourini told me you both woke up in the hospital a few days ago."

"That's right," confirmed Ernest "and we're grateful for all the attention you've been giving us."

"Instructor," Evelyn interrupted confidently "we've been hearing so much wild talk in our first few days here that I'd like to know whether we have the freedom to ask you anything, anything at all that could be causing us any sort of...."

"Oh, of course—ask anything. Can't guarantee that I'll have an answer, though."

She gave Ernest a significant look. Thus invited, the latter plunged in.

"Evelyn, from what I understand," he said, "has her mind fixed on a question of enormous importance. Now, this might seem like a childish idea to you—typical of mental patients, which we sometimes have the impression of being—but we've heard it said on various occasions that all of us here are dead and recuperating in a place that doesn't belong to the realm of the living. At first, we laughed at the idea, and considered it pure silliness. But more and more people keep assuring us that it's true. Even Mrs. Tambourini is certain that we've already crossed the barrier of death, like someone who has finished a night's sleep. What do you think, Instructor?"

Brother Claude's calm demeanor changed to one of deep reflection. "Would you be ready to accept my word for it," he said in a frank tone, "if I were to confirm for you that you are indeed perfectly alive in the Spiritual Plane?"

At these words, Evelyn turned pale. "But, Instructor...! " she cried.

"I see." Claude replied, smiling slightly. "Much more than our brother Ernest here, you're throwing up a strong mental defense against the truth. It comes, I know, from your religious beliefs—naturally, since they're such a large part of your spiritual constitution. Well, let me tell you, Evelyn, those convictions are very praiseworthy, but they also offer only a partial explanation. On the other hand, it's my duty to assure both of you that we're no longer walking on the Earth we're all so familiar with but in one of the regions of the Spiritual Life."

"My God, how can that be?" said Evelyn.

"Evelyn, use your own mind. We appeared on the planet's surface out of our mother's wombs, went through the infancy stage, and submitted ourselves to a long period of readaptation. Isn't this exactly the same thing?"

"But I know Earth."

"Purely a mistake. We look at Earth's environment

and its inhabitants through the prism of the ideas held by the people who came before us. The same thing happens here: we have our own noted geologists and geographers, you know. But actually, whether we're there or here we know essentially very little about the environment we find ourselves in. In a word, we analyze and reanalyze things and principles we find ready-made."

"Still, on Earth, as we understand it, we can be sure that we're standing on solid ground—that we have reference points in matter. "

"And who's convinced you, Evelyn, that when we lived on Earth we weren't equally certain of ideas concerning our eternal spirit? Any first-year science student over there can tell you that this so-called dense matter is just a compact form of energy. In the last analysis, we'll come to realize that matter is compressed light, a divine substance, suggesting the omnipresence of God."

Ernest asked, "Are you positively *confirming* then that we aren't living on the physical plane right now?"

"Whether we call the world we're living on at this moment the other life, the other side, the extra-physical region, or the plane of the spirit, our activity is just as material in its essence as that of our incarnate brothers and sisters, who move around conditioned by the kind of ideas and images that almost completely govern their sensory perceptions. Earth is what the thought of humankind makes it. Over here, it's the same thing. Matter is just energy. Both there and here, what we see is the temporary projection of our mental creations."

With some anxiety, Ernest asked, "What is death all about then? What purpose does it serve for us to recognize ourselves once we come back to consciousness?"

"The mysteries of life, with its challenges, are always the same. But if someone really wants to take the measure of life, then he or she will find this new world— with the study and rediscovery of self—full of very fascinating surprises. Each and every one of us, you see, is a sun of intelligence, looking into and perfecting ourselves."

Ernest kept the questions coming. "Are all dead people in all places on Earth," he asked, "in the same situation as we are?"

"Not possible. Let's take a quick look at incarnate humanity, and you'll get a better picture of the human situation. On Earth, where we came from, there are millions of spiritually stable, as well as spiritually unstable people—healthy ones and sick ones; knowledgeable ones and ignorant ones; some relatively spiritualized, others dragged down by extreme animalism. There are also the religious and the unbelievers, the ones who are relatively mature on the evolutionary path and the ones just beginning on it. To treat all these individuals alike—by the same standard—after death would be impractical. So each one of us naturally falls into his or her own group, and each group into its own community or what we would call its 'band of vibrational affinity'.

"It isn't easy to standardize the situation of disincarnate spirits, you know. Think of this: approximately 150,000 people per day, or 100 per minute, in today's terms, leave the Earth, which means that they're also leaving behind loved ones, accomplishments, debts, problems, etc. Well, we're all God's children, and receive the proper attention and right measures from God, just as we receive love from the Creator here—even if the ways we express it are different. It's also reasonable to accept that, no matter how our relatives dress us up and praise us once we say goodbye to the world, we arrive on this side, whoever we once were, exactly the way we truly are. Just because a lunatic has left his body behind doesn't mean he's going to become sane all of a sudden. Nor is the poorly educated person going to gain knowledge by some kind of osmosis. After death, we're what we made of ourselves, in our internal reality, and we put ourselves in places that are best-suited for recuperation, and for opportunities of service we might prove capable of doing."

"We have a lot of work in front of us then," commented Ernest, astonished at what he'd just heard.

"That's right. In the physical world, someone doesn't change immediately just because he crosses the ocean and goes from one continent to another. The same is true in the Spirit Domain."

"Some time ago," said Ernest "I read a message given by trustworthy spirits that described the sufferings and conflicts they had experienced in the lower regions. Those spirits seemed to be quite intellectually advanced, though."

"Quite true. Because of our own particular needs, we're living in one of those regions ourselves—in the vicinity of the incarnate."

"Actually I was thinking about the dark or unhappy regions. I've heard them described often; it's where so many of our brothers suffer. "

"Ernest, we have to realize that just because the spirits who live there are unhappy doesn't mean that there's something intrinsically bad about the region," the instructor explained. "Would the gardens and trees around an asylum be any less beautiful just because sick people are there, enjoying healing emanations?"

Ernest still looked confused.

"You see, my friend, the areas in space where suffering and unbalanced spirits live can sometimes be extensive, but they're always limited and strictly policed. They're like hospitals for the mentally ill on Earth. You know, there are spiritually sick people who spend a large part of their lives on Earth in asylums. The same thing happens here. For instance, our little village here is surrounded by a vast territory used to shelter thousands of maladjusted individuals. And there are many charitable organizations that take care of their needs and watch over them."

Evelyn, who didn't believe a word she was hearing, objected. "But—if we're on a spiritual plane," she asked, obviously displeased, "what are we supposed to make of all these buildings we're looking at? Their architecture is almost exactly like architecture on Earth."

"That's not really much to be surprised about when you consider that the buildings on the physical plane originate in the architects' *thoughts* and in the material that's used in the engineers' construction plans. The construction of our buildings follows the same principle, except that the matter is in a state much more malleable to the influence of thought. Just consider for a moment how much progress is being made on the physical plane now in the plastics industry. You can imagine, then, the enormous potential that exists for the construction of delicate and complex buildings in this world. It's a matter of having more clarity of thought. Of course, we're also limited to the techniques, trades, personal abilities, and creativity of each individual: it all depends on that individual's own spiritual advancement. The architect who plans a house and the worker who builds it can't, all of a sudden, replace the manager of a textile-manufacturing plant and the employee who helps her. And it isn't possible over here for a writer, by improvising, to do the job of a musician. We're all involved in a process of evolution and we haven't reached the level of multifaceted geniuses, even though those kinds of geniuses are here, too."

Evelyn couldn't hide her disbelief. "All this seems so—incredible," she said.

"Nothing is more incredible than the truth," Brother Claude replied. "But no matter how long we hold onto the illusion, reality remains what it is."

Evelyn was a woman of deep religious faith, and this subject was making her dizzy and fatigued. Temporarily she was unable to come up with better objections, so she took the opportunity of a break in the conversation to say, "Brother Claude, I don't doubt for a moment the sincerity of your beliefs. But it's hard for me to accept that we're disincarnated people, to use your expression. Now, I don't want to seem ungrateful for your instruction, but I'd like to be put in contact with a clergyman—a Catholic priest, for example. I'd be very pleased if I could go to confession and exchange ideas freely with some cleric who belongs to my faith. That faith formed my character."

Brother Claude smiled; a look of kindness and understanding crossed his face. "The Church here is definitely renewed," he said. "In the areas surrounding our community, where you'll find thousands of rebellious intelligences, you can find representatives of all the religions on Earth—individuals tied to narrow concepts and prejudices, and tyrannical leaders of various fanatic sects. But inside our walls the clergy won't listen to your confession, at least not one from a religious point of view. They'll send you to one of our institutes of mental health, where you'll see your personal files and receive the appropriate help."

Ernest asked, "For treatment, you mean?"

"For treatment—and assistance," said Brother Claude. "There you receive a medical card that gives you access to analysis and therapy services. In places like the one I'm referring to, where a person might be under long-term psychological supervision, the medical card is a very valuable document. It is the reference document that assures that person the proper healing assistance during this phase of adjustment. Keep in mind that we are in an environment that is intermediate between the lower and higher spiritual realms. I say proper assistance because it's crucial, at this stage, that we don't delve into painful memories without a clear purpose.."

"Oh! I see," said Ernest, enthusiastically. "I'm interested in this type of confession. If we are really dead. "

"Your *if*," interrupted the Instructor, smiling, "shows that you and Evelyn still consider me a storyteller, a fable spinner. Both of you are disembodied beings, and your roots are still firmly planted in earthly ground. Perfectly natural, of course. Let's give ourselves some more time, shall we?"

Waves of empathy and confidence passed among them and Ernest and Evelyn asked for the Instructor's help in making the necessary contacts with some of the city's psychotherapy institutes.

They agreed to pursue these contacts as soon as they got the necessary consent from hospital administration.

Chapter 10

EVELYN SERPA

Not long afterwards, Evelyn and Ernest received their permits, and after a quick trip through the city streets— which, they agreed, were enchanting—they arrived at the Institute of Spiritual Guidance. Seeing it, they relaxed immediately. The place looked like a modern doctor's office on Earth, crowded with filing cabinets, various odd-looking medical instruments, and attendants busy at their tasks. Everything was simplicity itself, comfortable and secure; nothing looked in the least out of place.

Instructor Rivas, assigned to the Department of Assistance dedicated to psychological care, met them, and after the introductions and handshaking were over, came straight to the subject at hand. "We're told that both of you plan to register with our office," he said. "We'll start with Sister Evelyn." He signaled to, and was immediately answered by an attendant he called Brother Telmo. Pointing to Ernest, he told Telmo, "They're together. I'll take Sister Evelyn first." Then, turning to Ernest, he said with a smile, "Don't worry. All our conversations at the Institute are geared toward encouragement and health. So—no negative thoughts! As soon as I finish interviewing our friend here, we'll have our own meeting."

The whole setting was so intimate and had such an air of spontaneity about it that the two newcomers could hardly believe the real situation. Were they really in the Spirit World, or were they still on Earth, the one familiar to them, but in a place they didn't know, where people used phrases like *liberated spirit* as a kind of psychological jargon, part of some new therapeutic procedure perhaps? They were almost ready to accept the notion that they had gone mad and were now in the process of recovering their senses.

Evelyn, with these doubts floating through her mind, followed the instructor meekly. They came to a room, simply and tastefully furnished, where at his prompting she sat down on the couch. The instructor started to explain: "Please stay calm. This Institute is dedicated to guiding and treating its clients. We usually start with crisis counseling and then behavior therapy if it's needed. Today, we're just going to have a little heart-to-heart chat. No standing on ceremony. We'll simply talk and our conversation will be recorded for future study. Actually, for all practical purposes, my role is to screen and become acquainted with our clients, who generally have a large support group of friends in the rearguard, so to speak. They examine the recorded words and reactions and will analyze the recording of each session. In this way we determine how and to what extent we can be of help."

The instructor made a motion with his hand, and before Evelyn's astonished eyes, a large mirror became visible next to the couch. Some special device, she thought, must be connecting the mirror to the electrical system.

"Our conversation will be recorded on video," Instructor Rivas told her. "It's simply a resource we use to ensure that your sessions follow the proper procedures. We want to be sure that you get all the assistance you're entitled to during the initial stages of your spiritual life. So stay calm, but please understand that all the questions and answers are intended to bring about the greatest possible benefit to you. According to your own questions, the Institute will be able to identify your level of understanding, and by your answers we'll get to know the level of your needs."

The instructor's expression was at once gentle and energetic, but Evelyn recoiled a bit, like a first grader confronted by an experienced test-giver. Since she realized that she wouldn't be allowed to refuse the test, she summoned her courage and asked politely, "Instructor Rivas, despite your reference to my *initial stages of spiritual life*, is it true that we're disincarnate spirits, people who don't live on Earth any more?"

"Absolutely—despite your inability to verify this at the moment."

"Why this inability?"

"Lack of preparation during the physical life. This astonishment you feel is actually fairly common to people from Earth because they've never fully realized and integrated their religious experience into their lives, even though they devoted themselves to it."

"Then if we're truly *dead*, do you believe that, as a Catholic, I must present or should be presenting a greater level of communion with spiritual truth, although I can't seem to understand it right now?"

"Obviously."

"How so?"

"If during your earthly existence you had thought carefully about the teachings of Jesus, the Divine Master who raised Himself from the tomb to demonstrate eternal life; and if you had meditated on the essence of the rituals of your faith—all directed toward God first, and then, to the sublime dead, such as Our Lord Jesus Christ, His glorious Mother, and the heroic spirits we venerate as Christian saints—you wouldn't, I assure you, be so shaken. The truth is that this circumstance has temporarily deadened your spiritual energy centers, even though you are a person of elevated and sensitive feelings." She remembered the prayers, the hymns, the novenas, the religious liturgies. But only now, in this blessed therapy room, was she able to unlock the real meaning of all those acts. Why did it never dawn on her to consider them as invitations to reflect about the world beyond? How in the world could she not have seen them as ways to come into contact with the Divine Forces? In thought, she wished herself back in São Paulo,

able to walk to church and once again celebrate her con-
secration to the Almighty. It was there that she was able
to really trust herself and all her troubles, joys, sufferings, and fears, to God. She remembered Jesus—in the
sculptures and on the panels, in the preaching and conversations—as the Divine Spirit knocking in vain at her
heart's door, trying to teach her how to live and to understand. Now she reflected on the Master of infinite
patience, on whose great goodness she had always re-
lied during moments of trial and tribulation. Yet she had
never bothered to search His lessons diligently or follow His examples. As she thought about these things,
she started to cry. She felt as if the Christian faith, so
sublime and reverent, had changed in that moment into
a judge in the recesses of her soul, reproaching her.

She cried out, "Oh, my Lord! Why did I have to *die*
to understand? Why, Lord? Why?"

There she was, exposing her soul, talking about
herself, rendering an account of herself. What did she
bring, in her own life baggage, but the emptiness of an
existence that was, she thought, useless? Yet it seemed
to her, too, that the mental blocks that had isolated her
from eternal realities were now suddenly dissolved—
that they were lost in the lightness of thought in which
she was immersed. It was as if Jesus, whom she adored
externally, was now conquering the privacy of her heart,
asking her with infinite sweetness, "Evelyn, what have
you done with Me?"

Upset, she cried convulsively in front of the instructor. Greatly moved, Rivas watched over her with the

care of a father. He let her have her fill of crying and then said, once she had calmed down, "This temporary pain will do you good, Evelyn. The pain of conscience can serve as a measure of our notion of responsibility. Your sorrow, remembering Our Lord Jesus, demonstrates your faith in Him."

In a more tender tone, Instructor Rivas now gave a new direction to the analysis. He let Evelyn know that her identification file was ready. Even before her arrival, he told her, the Health Institute, through which she had entered the city, had been consulted about her origins and parentage on Earth. He then added, "Your deposition here, however, will be very valuable. It will give us more information about the assistance we should give you."

"Can you tell me what kind it will be?"

"Yes, we'll be able to evaluate it from your answers."

"But, Instructor, doesn't anyone in the Spirit World know me? Don't all of us have guardians in our earthly existence?"

"Precisely. Everyone who knows us has a certain version of our experiences for their own use. In this analysis, however, your personal version is very important, since your autobiographical notes will come directly from your own conscience. We have to promote a self-encounter in the area of the soul's reality. It will let us determine your immediate needs more exactly. Of course, in other places, you'll show up in the files of your friends and acquaintances—at least, the impression you made on them will show up. But, at the Institute, we'll extract your individual and untransferable projection."

His client was now in a state of expectation as well as amazement, so the instructor began by asking her to remember, aloud, a few instances from her own history, starting with her most distant memory. She should avoid an exhaustive report, and try as much as possible to summarize her experiences.

Evelyn, speaking in a soft and humble voice, started to talk about her life. "My memories start a little bit confusedly, around the time I lost my father. I was a very young child, and one day I heard my mother screaming. She held me close to her and told me I was now an orphan. Not long afterwards she married again. My stepfather was a good, friendly man but, after the marriage, both he and my mother decided to leave the area where we were living—probably trying to put painful memories behind them. The man who became the head of our household was tender in his feelings toward me but, instinctively, I always missed my father. I could never find out much information about him and was never able to find out any more from my mother than that he had died suddenly, while on a trip. As I grew older, I understood that my mother refused to talk about the past as a way of avoiding possible conflicts with her husband—who, to tell you the truth, always treated her with great love.

"When I was twelve years old, I started attending a Catholic boarding school for girls. I graduated as a teacher, but never worked because, by the time my senior year Prom rolled around, two young men, Túlio Mancini and Caio Serpa, had each proposed to me. Well, I was very young and irresponsible, and I admit I allowed my heart to shift back and forth between the two of them. I committed myself to both of them at once. Then, when I finally became engaged to Caio, Túlio tried to commit suicide. Eventually, I saw that he was out of danger, and I changed my mind and came back to him. But just as I was about to ask Caio to let me out of the engagement, Túlio did commit suicide. He shot himself through the heart.

"After this terrible event, I married Caio, and for a few months we were happy. Only one thing frustrated us; we couldn't seem to have a child. I did get pregnant, but soon afterwards I had a therapeutic abortion on recommendation of my physician. Following that, I became progressively weaker. And there's one more thing: maybe it was because of my illness, but Caio found someone else, a single young woman, and he started a love affair with her. It was a shameful situation, and it devastated me. The constant humiliation I was exposed to inside my own home made me bitter.

"Beyond that, I don't have anything else to report, except my own moral suffering and the lack of will to live, because of the sickness you're treating me for today."

The instructor gazed at her, touched once again, and asked, "Have you forgiven your husband for cheating on you, and did you take pity on your rival?"

Evelyn thought for a few moments and answered

bitterly, "Absolutely not. I'm confessing and I take Jesus as my witness, so I can't lie. But I've never been able to forgive Caio for betraying me, and I could never tolerate the presence of the *other* one in our path."

The instructor was not, as Evelyn feared he might be, angry at this admission. Instead, he said affectionately, "We understand your human feelings, so let's end today's session. You have difficult problems to resolve, and our Institute will see how much support it'll be able to give you. We'll stay in contact and continue our conversation in the future."

Evelyn left the room then, and Ernest came in to begin his own session.

Chapter 11

ERNEST FANTINI

E rnest, his turn having come, took the seat Evelyn had just vacated. He was feeling a little bewildered. The instructor gave him the same instructions he'd given Evelyn, asking him to pose questions. Then Rivas turned on the recording mirror.

In a few moments, Ernest felt more at ease and started his inquiry.

"May I speak as if I were really dead, as you make me believe I am?"

The instructor smiled at these words from such an intelligent materialist. He answered softly: "Say anything you want, but with the conviction that your theory of *as if* is far away from us now. We're definitely out of the material body, trying to find ourselves."

"Instructor, if I left my body on Earth, without remembering that I did, isn't it true that on returning to the natural environment of the Spirit—this place—I'd remember the time I once lived here as a free spirit, that is, before I began wearing the body I just left behind among the living? Why doesn't this happen?"

"Look at it this way. The body is a vehicle we use for learning or healing ourselves, for self-redemption, or for accomplishing a specific task. But it also drives us into the energy conditioning within which we operate in the world. It drives us to do what we *must* do. Now, don't misunderstand me. Where consciousness is concerned, free will remains in effect and unchanged. No matter what position an incarnate being finds itself in during its period of incarnation, it's always free to choose its own path. But during this period the other latent capabilities of the soul remain oriented to one task or another, depending on the goals the soul set for itself before its physical existence—or had to accept. This is what determines the forgetfulness of previous incarnations—a forgetfulness that is, in any event, temporary. This temporary period can be relatively short or long, according to the degree of spiritual evolution the spirit has already made."

"As if we had suffered, during our stay in the physical plane, a period of prolonged amnesia?"

"Yes, up to a point. The stay in the womb, the new name we're given, the first seven years of semi-consciousness spent in the love field of the parents, the re-living of childhood, the return to adolescence, the problems of adulthood with its responsibilities and duties, form in us, even as we remain the same essential being, a new personality that we incorporate into our collective experiences. It's understandable that during the period immediately following the death of the physical body, the inner memory of these personalities is tightly stored in the innermost recesses of the living being. However, as I say, this is just transitory. Gradually, we regain control of our memories."

"You mean, then, that in this city, I'm still Ernest Fantini, the human personality with the name given to me during the life I just ended, and that I should leave the study of my previous incarnations for later on?"

"Exactly. Each of us stays here, very near the physical plane, as part of a renewal workgroup, and with the same identity as the one we recently had there. Until we get ourselves transferred to higher circles of sublimation, we live our time between the high mountains of spirituality and the lowlands of the physical life— working continuously on improving ourselves—threading the path that includes the birth in the cradle, the rebirth in death, and the analysis in the spirit realm, and back again. Do you understand?"

"So, over here we're evaluated by what we were, by the actions taken during the time we spent on Earth."

"That's it precisely."

"We are here what we made of ourselves there, exactly the characters our personal records paint, until..."

"Until circumstances suggest new opportunities, new reasons for entering into a new carnal body. That body is a resource, a necessary one that helps us achieve the goals we all have during the toils of our journey."

"We are as we were, even down to the very form and structure of our old organism?"

"Ah, now you're talking about morphology! The answer is, not quite. Any morphological characteristic can be changed by the condition of the mind and how it's organized. In the Land of the Living, this happens often. Science, without much difficulty, can alter an individual's genetically produced machinery according to his or her psychological tendencies as a way of trying to harmonize the body/mind duality. And we shouldn't forget advances in plastic surgery. Doctors can now perform veritable miracles in changing the way people look, when they merit such improvements. All this, of course, is made possible by the medical sciences on Earth. A very generous and optimistic enterprise, don't you think?"

Ernest was pleasantly surprised by the instructor's mental agility and the way he communicated his clarifications, filling up a head anxious for enlightenment. "Instructor Rivas," he asked, "I've already talked about the subject with Brother Claude, but I'd like to know what you have to say, too. I've heard that some individuals, even very well-educated ones, spend years after death in inferior zones, living in torment before they can regain their clarity of mind and sense of calm. If I'm really without a physical body, and also aware of my own failings, why didn't this happen to me?"

"The kind of trial you're referring to has to do with the state of the spirit and not with the place. A lot of us in the spirit state, Ernest, go through hard times in landscapes that reflect our own internal problems. The situation can last a long time, depending on our tendencies, the effort we decide to put into accepting ourselves with all our imperfections, and the extent to which we realize the necessity for self-improvement, which is one of the laws of life. For now, we are consciences in debt. To put it another way, we have been following an evolutionary road that has come short of the Great Life— so we have the duty of pruning our defects. That pruning is done through worthwhile and constant work. After our physical life, and as long as we are in a state of mental imbalance which can be aggravated by our nonconformity or rebellion, by our pride and desperation— all of which threaten others' security—we have to stay, and understandably so, interned or segregated in certain areas with spirits who are as disturbed and full of conflicts as we are. Just like mental patients who are taken out of the home situation so they can get proper treatment."

"So, the idea of *punishment from God...*"

"Is reasonable, until we learn that Divine Providence governs us through wise and impartial laws. We punish ourselves according to the articles of the Divine Statutes we broke. Eternal Justice works in our internal forum—the conscience, you understand—which determines, according to the extent of our knowledge, what responsibility we have to accept for our thoughts and actions."

"Does the idea of hell then, which religions so often preach on Earth, actually refer to this condition of the soul?"

"Let's give this topic the respect it demands. After

all, to millions of souls, the mental discomfort they experience is perfectly compatible with the theological hell thought up by the various human beliefs. To be exact, however—and keeping in mind the fact that God never abandons us—hell should be interpreted as an asylum where we suffer the consequences of our wrong-doing, which in the end we committed against ourselves. It's easy to see that the areas we stay in while we're in this bleak situation come to reflect the unfortunate mental pictures we create and project around us."

"I ask so many questions," admitted Ernest, "because I'm absolutely convinced I don't deserve the generosity I've received here. I've enjoyed a peace of mind here I didn't expect, considering the burden of guilt I carry."

"It's precisely one of the functions of our Institute to support those who come here with guilt complexes but with their moral integrity intact and strong enough to push them to change in positive ways. We're more effective, of course, when the individual believes that he or she can overcome particular weaknesses. Now, in your case, you have a psychological structure that has immunized you against the illusions of many good and smart people—people who sometimes stay for a long time in the big asylums we talked about while they undergo the cleansing of suffering. These people create that situation in the process of healing the imbalances that are caused, many times, by a false orientation to a love they've nourished."

Instructor Rivas allowed a slight pause. Then, with

a smile, he continued: "Despite your admirable level of resistance, you're not sure about the results of your own actions and must brace yourself to confront them."

"What do you mean?"

"That you have to develop inner strength in order to face the problems you left in the world. It's the only way to understand them and yourself. In the physical plane, we sometimes hear that it takes courage to see and hear the dead. Well, the situation here isn't that different in relation to the living. In general, all of us, after death, attend classes in order to attain a basic level of spiritual understanding. In these we gain enough will power to allow us to revisit the living and see and hear them again, without hurting them or us."

As he considered this explanation, Ernest's eyes grew wide. Thick tears ran down his cheeks. It was as if he were suffering from the pressure of invisible coils that were forcing him to spill the guilt gnawing away at him.

In another moment he knelt down like a frightened child.

"Instructor Rivas," he cried, "I believe I only have one debt; but it's enough to make up for many hells in my spirit. Over twenty years ago, I killed a friend and since then I've had no peace. I knew this man was after my wife. He would look at her in ways that gave away his intentions—following her every move, being overly attentive to her needs. Once, while I was out, I saw him spying on my house. At times, I heard him say what I considered suspicious things to her. One day, I had the impression that my wife was looking at this man in a way that told me she had feelings for him. Unfortunately, I didn't take the time to confirm my suspicions. I did take advantage of a favorable moment, though, and shot him while we were out quail hunting together. I hid myself in the bushes, and after a while another hunting friend who was with us came along and found the body. The victim had hit the ground in a way that his death looked like a hunting accident, and everyone accepted that explanation. I pretended to accept it, too—frightened by my crime as I was—but from that moment I was never able to have peace. The man I killed was also married, but I didn't have the courage to look for his family. They left the area soon afterward, trying to forget the terrible accident. I, on the other hand, couldn't forget it. The death I had caused seemed to have brought my enemy right inside my house. I started to feel his presence, in the form of a constant shadow, always mocking and insulting me—though nobody else noticed it. At home, I found myself handcuffed to him, as if the damned specter was still alive and getting stronger every day. It was a rare night that I didn't fight with him in my dreams, that is, before the surgery that brought me here. I'd wake up exhausted, as if I had just fought a mortal duel. I kept on seeing him, in my imagination, still sharing my daily life. Oh, Instructor Rivas, Instructor Rivas! In God's name, tell me if there's a solution for me! After death I expected to find a place of punishment where infernal powers would try to collect the debt I hid from justice on Earth. But now the care I'm enjoying here only adds to my inner torment. What's going to become of me? I can't stand myself."

So saying, Ernest threw his arms around the instructor and cried like a helpless boy begging for shelter. The instructor, in return, hugged him sympathetically. "Be calm, my son," he said consolingly. "We're eternal spirits, and God won't leave us without help."

Rivas's eyes were full of tears that didn't fall. He, the competent counselor, knew firsthand the pain of conscience Ernest was undergoing and, far from finding fault, he caressed the tired head.

"God's Justice doesn't come without Mercy," he said. "We must have faith!"

Then he got up, still touched by the scene, turned off the recording mirror, and declared the session over.

Chapter 12

JUDGMENT AND LOVE

A few weeks passed, and Ernest and Evelyn had begun to feel less awkward in their new surroundings. They continued to treasure their friendship, and were growing steadily closer to each other. The health of each had improved markedly. They continued, however, to stay at the hospital, though now in the convalescent wing—which was, in fact, a large apartment complex, with individual units for men and women. They now had almost unrestricted freedom of movement, though they were advised not to venture into the outskirts, where thousands of troubled individuals gathered, unless accompanied by a staff member.

In the meantime, both were beginning to feel the need for work, disciplined and regular, in some meaningful capacity. Yet when they asked for it or some other activity in their former homes—which neither had been able to visit yet—the answer was always the same: "Wait just awhile longer. First you have to undergo a preparation period. It's indispensable." This being the case, they visited the city's libraries, gardens, institutions, and took in various types of entertainment. Life, it seemed to them, had become an extended vacation.

One day, however, one of Evelyn's deepest wishes became a reality. Ernest had promised to take her, after getting the necessary consent from their mentors, to an evening worship service, which was to consist of a sermon entitled "Judgment and Love." The opportunity excited both of them, anxious as they were to have a closer look at how religious activities were carried out in this new and beautiful world.

So it was that they set out together on the evening of their appointed outing. During their walk, Evelyn remembered her visits, in other times, to the sanctuary of her own faith, and held in her heart the warmest and sweetest recollections of them. Moved, she thought, "Why did I lose contact with my family, and why am I in the company of someone I met on Earth only once?"

A calm breeze carried toward them the scent of flowers from the surrounding gardens; and the moon, shining on the horizon, was the same majestic and beautiful spectacle she knew on Earth. From time to time, Evelyn exchanged a word with Ernest, and watched other parties strolling in the same direction.

After a few minutes of this happy pilgrimage, the two found themselves facing a temple. In its simplicity, it was a remarkable building, resembling an enormous dove cote, covered by a translucent coating of snow and protected here and there by thickets of trees. Inside, everything was harmony and spontaneity. A long line of benches provided a good view of the pulpit, which was shaped like a huge lilac and sculpted from dazzling white marble. On the white walls facing the congregation were two signs: "Temple of the New Revelation" and "House Consecrated to Our Lord Jesus Christ." There were no symbols or sculptures—only a screen on which the features of the Divine Master were displayed. In this fine picture, His eyes seemed to speak of life and His own omnipresence.

Seated by Ernest, Evelyn glanced quickly around at the faces of the others in the congregation—some calm, others anxious in appearance—who sat near her in complete silence. Then she found herself deep in prayer.

Suddenly, as if he had materialized at the rostrum or perhaps only entered through a hidden door, a man appeared, dressed in a white tunic. Reverently, he greeted the assembly and, looking upward, began a moving prayer in which he asked Jesus's blessings on the waiting audience. Then, he moved toward a large copy of the New Testament, which lay open on top of a delicate book stand, and read Matthew 7: 1-4.

"Do not judge, or you too will be judged. For in the same way you judge others, you will be judged, and with the measure you use, it will be measured to you.

Why do you look at the speck of sawdust in your brother's eye and pay no attention to the plank

in your own eye? How can you say to your brother,
'Let me take the speck out of your eye,' when all the
time there is a plank in your own eye?"

The reading finished, the minister fell silent and remained so for a period of what seemed prolonged concentration. It was as if he were looking into the depths of his own soul for inspiration. To their surprise, however, Ernest and Evelyn noticed that the direction of his thoughts had to be the other way around. Rather than rising from within, these thoughts materialized in the form of a large halo of light around his head like a flame. The halo continued to rise steadily, and seconds later, waves of light came down from above, like the tongues of fire at Pentecost. Thereafter, the good priest began his sermon.

"Brothers and sisters, not long ago we were all an integral part of the human collective—that is to say, our beloved family on the physical plane—and we believed firmly there in our right to judge one another. Ensconced in religious beliefs, which we imagined sanctioned our passions, we came to hate as evil and corrupt anyone who dared to differ from us.

"We interpreted the teachings of Our Lord Jesus Christ just as we pleased, and even commanded that the Master of Life become, on that dark, tortuous road we were following, our humble servant. Today, with that body of dense matter, which so encouraged our illusions, stripped away, we've learned that we're all consciousness and that each of us has flaws before the Law. We now understand that, for our own good, only the Lord has the resources to judge us fairly—for, in truth, we are not competent to judge anyone.

"What we were in the deepest recesses of our hearts on Earth, we are here as well. But in this generous refuge—where the Lord allows us to live temporarily—we understand, without being forced by anyone, that the devices we used to mask our own reality in the material world (so that we could play our required roles in human affairs) have now been taken away from us. We are then, in this sphere of spiritual reality, who we really are, composed of all the good and bad qualities we acquired during our sojourn on Earth.

"Many of you still have the same habits and hold on to the same misconceptions as in the carnal experience. Gradually you will lose these, however, because in this environment they lack any real importance. Your mansions or shacks, your fancy titles or contemptible credits, your privileges or privations, your family honors or plebeian bloodlines, the advantages or disadvantages of your looks, all the mental conditioning that led you to assume certain rights or imagine complaints, together with the abandonment of the natural duty to spiritual development in preparation for eternal life, have disappeared. They disappeared the day you left the physical plane. Afterwards, those you left behind signed your death certificate, took control of your assets, analyzed your actions, and then, in many cases, let you slip from their thoughts in the mistaken belief that they could banish you from their memories forever.

"How many of you have come here to fathom the truth that you closed your ears to so often on Earth? Divine Providence doesn't ask what you were, because it knows at every moment. But it's only right that you investigate what you did with the treasures of time that you, and all of us, receive in equal amounts. The better educated ones among you should ask yourselves how you applied your gifts of knowledge. The less educated, where you applied your time. The rich should ask what kind of work you did that made your money worthwhile. Those without money, but often rich in other gifts, what you did with your opportunities to practice patience and service, insight and humbleness of heart. You young ones should ask what you used your strength for. You older ones, turned gray by time, what good deeds the glow of your better understanding led you to.

"Don't fool yourselves! Like those of us who've been living in the Spiritual Plane for decades now, you brought over here what you made of yourselves over there. Here you are skilled at what you studied there, you show what you accomplished, you accumulate what you gave away! In short, in crossing the Great Frontier, you simply are what you were! You'll understand then, as you live your daily life in this dwelling place of sublime realities, that all the disguises that covered your real individuality in the world will wane naturally, and what had been on Earth your innermost life will be revealed. Once the restrictions of the flesh go, each spirit reveals itself. Automatically, in this ancestral home of the soul, we're stamped with the attitudes and words, the thoughts and feelings, that are peculiarly ours. We can't resort to subterfuges any more.

"In manifesting all we are and all we have in the recesses of our beings, the hour of judgment must come for each of us. But the Divine Mercy of Our Lord offers us this home base—which, like so many other places in the Spiritual Realm, is a waiting-room for introspection and service. Here we find valuable preparation for our ascent to the Greater Life. We are in one of the outlying provinces of that Life now, and have to apply ourselves to attain the necessary victories in the ongoing and blessed fight for our own betterment.

"However, in this climate of renewal where we're all living, those of you who still reject the sublime opportunities of time will certainly, at your own will, retreat to our far-off districts. There you'll find agents of turmoil and darkness—spirits who relish their own sickness and treat each other cruelly, according to the unfortunate law of 'an eye for an eye.' Eventually, these individuals will get tired of rebelling, and plead for the mercy of Eternal Laws. What they ask for is the precious gift of a reincarnation. That gift will allow them to renew themselves through arduous trials on Earth, and at length they will return to these grounds—but God alone knows when!

"We're not trying, by saying these things, to say that rebirth in the physical arena is always the crucible where we make amends for our past wrong-doing. There are among us here thousands of friends, who, after long and honest effort in self-transformation and after spending a great deal of time serving this community, go back to the physical world. There they do work that often calls for self-denial and anonymous heroism. They will live next to someone or within a group of people with the same problems; and, in an anonymity that's praiseworthy, they win concessions and victories of enormous value. Once back here these spirits, despite often being ignored by humankind, celebrate their transformation, having earned the purification passes that grant them access to higher planes.

Here, bathed in an intense light, the orator paused. Evelyn and Ernest exchanged glances, and quickly looking around them, noticed that dozens of faces were drenched in tears.

"Brothers and sisters," the minister continued, "don't think you're in a court of law when you're in a house of faith! Faith is the loving mother of our pursuit of betterment and elevation. Faith points out to us, in this calm and activity-rich corner, that despite being disincarnate, we have to recognize that our opportunities for work and progress, self-correction and learning, haven't ended.

"Let's accept ourselves as we truly are, recognize the size of our debts, and set to work helping our brothers and sisters faithfully, without looking back. This community has plenty of service institutions with open doors. Those institutions need volunteers who want to cooperate by assisting those who daily come to us in situations of anguish or need. On Earth, where our families continue fighting the hard battles of evolution, our loved ones demand from us testimonies of love in the form of spiritual support. In that way they can continue their earthly experiences as happier and more tranquil individuals, though we aren't there with them physically. For most of you, a veritable apostolate of constructive self-giving, tenderness, and understanding will open in your own earthly homes, where the majority still have bonds!

"In addition, we're surrounded here by multitudes of troubled comrades, who beg for love and patience during their recuperation. In the physical arena, we used to send countless appeals for food and clothing for the hungry and needy. Here, we're challenged to provide and sustain devotion and tolerance, so that harmony and understanding can take hold in the suffering and troubled souls of those lost in the darkness of spirit.

"Charity, brothers and sisters! Love your neighbor! Many times, a few days of service will allow us to borrow energies and means, as we struggle to recuperate and elevate ourselves, that would require many years of effort on our part.

"Let us pray then, asking our Lord to inspire us on the road of purification that goes through new and blessed opportunities on Earth, or to lead us on the pathways of sublimation in the spiritual kingdom."

The minister stopped and began to pray silently. Soon he was in a state of deep meditation. Small petals, in color like the light of many sapphires, fell through the ceiling, dissolving gently as they touched the heads of the congregation, or disappearing the instant they touched the ground. From the minister's chest a silvery, translucent star seemed to form. From its center came a torrent of white rays, which flooded the entire room.

Ernest was deeply moved. Evelyn, like so many of their fellows in the congregation, couldn't stop sobbing. Tears came in growing waves from her heart to her eyes. She didn't know how to explain all this emotion—so sensitive had she become that it took immediate hold in the recesses of her heart. Nor could she have said whether these blessed tears were because of her aspirations to reach Heaven or her homesickness for Earth.

The minister closed the service for the night, but she didn't hear his last words. She only knew that she now needed the full support of Ernest's arm as she left the place, still crying.

Chapter 13

NEW TASKS

E rnest and Evelyn were deeply touched by the talk they had heard at the temple, and soon asked to join the relief caravan Brother Claude led on weekly visits to the region of their disturbed and suffering fellow spirits.

Claude answered the request positively, indeed with empathy and kindness. Thus in a few days the two friends found themselves traveling with an active service team of eight persons, five men and three women— among them, Mrs. Tambourini. The team was moving, on this pilgrimage of friendship, toward an extensive valley. Their goal, on this particular day, was to attend the Gospel At Home[9] gathering hosted by Ambrosio and Priscilla—a couple stationed, like many other guardians, along the border of the zone, where they battled the

---

[9]Translator's Note: Gospel At Home: weekly family meetings for the purpose of studying the Gospel and prayer.

mental projections of unbalanced souls.

The moment Ernest and Evelyn got a better view of the panorama before them, they gasped in amazement. A thick fog, various in its shades of grey, created a barrier along the entire border. For the first time, they noticed airborne transportation apparatuses, just arrived from the city, land in this dark territory. The craft, made of a subtle substance, looked like large and silent butterflies with the sun reflecting on their rainbow-colored wings.

"What are they?" Ernest asked, and Claude answered happily, "They're space transportation units. We have work teams devoted to first contact and assistance here, and it's the team members who use them."

"Is the region that large?"

"Imagine a desert on Earth distributed over a large area and bordered by prosperous, orderly cities, and you'll get an idea of our situation here."

"And these air travelers—they're spirits, of course. Can't they fly back and forth under their own power?"

The leader smiled and thought for a moment. "Everything in life is regulated by laws," he said. "On Earth, a bird has wings and flies away from a burning field because it can't stand the smoke. A firefighter wears special protective clothes in order to enter a house on fire. It's not so different with us. We find ourselves facing a very difficult stretch of space here—a space populated by thousands of rebellious individuals. Because of their deranged minds, they've created this desolate environment here themselves. It's a different world. In it we'll see some very strange buildings, all caricatures of the homes their owners abused during their physical lives. In fact, these buildings reflect the ideas and fixations, the ambitions and fancies, the regrets and repentances, of their dwellers. In this shadowy zone, a veritable state of anarchy is in force. An extreme individualism has led to an abnormal degree of license. The inhabitants lack the beneficial constraints of discipline. And discipline—the voluntary observation of God's laws—is what makes us really free."

Ernest asked, indulging in human logic, "And why does God let these huge, open sores exist?"

"Ah, Ernest," Brother Claude answered mildly. "All the time we ask our Elders why Divine Providence doesn't interfere in an area where intelligence is so corrupted by evil. The answer is always that the Creator requires that each creature be allowed to choose the evolutionary path that best suits it, whether the path is a starry or a muddy one. Providence wants every creature to have its own individuality, to believe in God as best it can, to use its inclinations and tastes to live in harmony with its way of being, to work however and how much it wants, and to live wherever it wants. God only demands—and demands rigorously—that justice be done and respected. 'To each shall be given according to his deeds.' According to the Laws of Life, all of us will receive according to what we have done, how much we've done, and how we've done it. We can conform to Divine Precepts and live together with one another, according to our own standards of choice and affection.

But, in any plane of consciousness from highest to lowest, hurting and offending others, wrong-doing, thanklessness, all bring about painful and inevitable corrections. Why? Because of the law of action and reaction which imposes on lawbreakers appropriate penalties. We're free to develop, cultivate, and perfect our own tendencies. But these tendencies have to be in accordance with the Statutes of the Eternal Good, which tell us they must be developed and maintained for the good of all, and in the unselfish support of others. These are guarantees of our own good."

They had now reached the dark outskirts of an odd-looking village. Here and there a few bewildered individuals showed up. To Ernest and Evelyn, they did not quite resemble the tramps one sees in the public places of Earth cities. They were more akin to beings whose pride or indifference had made them spiritually aloof.

Another group wore mocking expressions on their faces, suggesting sarcasm and contempt. Nearly all of them were dressed in strange clothes, each according to the condition and station in life to which they believed they belonged.

Ernest asked a question about them, and since he and Evelyn were the only newcomers to the relief team, Claude replied, "Generally, the thousands of people who live hereabouts don't accept themselves as they really are. They're so used to the pretenses of their earthly lives—which are sometimes necessary there—that the truth offends them. They lived for years and years on the carnal plane, infatuated with it, enjoying considerations of one kind or another because in a superficial way they were valued. Now they can't tolerate the crumbling of their illusions or losing the imaginary privileges they clung to once. Each one is like Narcissus; fixated on his or her own image just as they were on the physical plane. Many of them come to this foggy region directly from the physical life. Others, soon after disincarnation, lived in cities of recuperation and training like ours. But to the extent that they denied what they really are, and refused to give up the pretenses they used on Earth to hide their true selves, they rebelled against the light of the spirit world. That light, you see, exposed them to their true nature, one to another, so they ran away from our communities, looking for asylum in this valley. Once here, they generated these shadows. Yes, that's right, the shadows are created by their own mental force for the purpose of hiding themselves. In the shadows they feed on the paranoia they suffer from, indulging their passions, which can be—well—deplorable. They try to find satisfaction in these passions, but it's no use. Often the attempt drives them mad."

Evelyn asked, "You've been to these places often then, Brother Claude—the ones far away from the border?"

"Yes, I've traveled with many relief caravans like this one, using one kind of transportation or another. I've been to places a long way from here."

"And what did you see?"

"Towns, small villages, various settlements," he an-

swered with a sad smile. "And I've met individuals of
great culture and high intelligence there, too, but they
were depraved beings. They rule over large communities of souls that are just as perverted as their leaders."
He paused a moment, and then said, "Of course, when
I use the word perverted, I don't mean to be judgmen-
tal. They are being held in the shadows only for the time
being. I simply want to qualify, since you just came from
the physical life, the position of our sick friends; and
we do consider them sick—as sick as our brothers and
sisters in psychiatric wards on Earth—and worthy of
our highest respect. We also have to remember (and respect them for it) that many of the parents, spouses, sons,
daughters, and loved ones of our lost friends in these
shadowy regions, live here out of devotion. They're
unsung heroes, apostles of love and self-denial—very
admirable—and they do what they can to benefit their
loved ones who hold onto their old and mistaken beliefs. They try to lead them back to the necessary equilibrium, from which point they can prepare themselves
for new reincarnations. These souls form an army of
kindness and patience. But they do seem at times to be
slaves to the poor creatures. Still, this office of sacrifice,
this humility they have, ends up performing miracles
at times by the sheer force of their example."

Ambrosio's modest house could be seen in the distance. Ernest, as if trying not to lose the thread of the
conversation, asked another question, "Brother Claude,
is the number of spirits who are rescued from here in
this way usually high?"

"No doubt. Every day both small and large groups of individuals seeking renewal arrive outside our doors."

"And do they stay in the city permanently?"

"No. With very few exceptions, they stay with us only until they're ready for a new reincarnation—the return to the carnal envelope. Without it, they don't think they'll progress on the path of self-renewal. They get tired of wandering in the shadows of the mind, you see. And between that and terror of spiritual light, which they can't stand without long preparation, they pray to the Divine for providential help. Divine Providence then allows them a new period of internship on Earth. They again put on the physical armor in order to resume the struggle for their own self-correction and betterment. Then, little by little, the flesh envelope they have temporarily covered themselves in will wear out and reveal again the good and bad they did to themselves during that incarnation. So they receive new bodies, usually living close to their old partners in excess, or with people who have the same type of debts and are undergoing the same type of expiation. Only this time they take the initiative of asking for constraints in their lives. These may include home environments which will help them counter their inclinations, or new bodies in which certain functions will have limited expression. In other words, they take measures beforehand against inferior tendencies that, in the past, caused them to fall."

"You mean they ask for certain handicaps," said Ernest, showing his usual sharpness of mind.

"Yes, handicaps. And as a result, we find everywhere on Earth great talents frustrated because their owners can't take them in the direction they want to go. We see, for instance, individuals with powerful intellects barred, early on, from getting any academic degrees. Instead, they find themselves working in menial jobs, and going through long and unhappy periods of subordination—in the course of which, however, they acquire humility and equilibrium, peace and moderation. Or we come across artists whose highest hopes are disappointed—people who have physical defects and inhibitions that temporarily prevent their artistic gifts from being realized. Under those conditions, their impulses, particularly the ones relating to their respect for the feelings of others, are re-educated. Or we see women capable of great affection but tied to ugly bodies so they can learn, in terrible conflicts of the soul, how painful it is to abandon homes and show contempt for motherhood. Or we'll discover able and energetic men carrying within them insidious and occult frustrations that prevent them from enjoying physical pleasures as a way of building up their own spirit with awareness and love."

Suddenly this wonderful conversation—an unforgettable lesson—was interrupted. Ambrosio and Priscilla, who were waiting outside their home, came rushing up to the visitors and hugged each in turn. The team exchanged greetings, blessings, and well wishes, then went inside for the service.

The service was typical of the Gospel At Home practice found in Christian homes on Earth. Yet, in this humble abode, a valuable work of spiritual support to

the suffering spirits of the neighborhood was being extended. Twenty-two of these spirits , twenty women and
two men, had come from the great fog nearby to hear
Brother Claude speak—revealing their eagerness for
inner peace and greater awareness.

The service was along lines similar to evangelical
meetings on Earth. In addition, it had the well-known
Christian Spiritist orientation, which provides such a
respectful and yet free interpretation of the teachings
of Our Lord Jesus Christ. At the end of the meeting,
magnetic energy healing brought comfort and messages
of clarification, caution, and tenderness to the gathering. Ernest and Evelyn also found their own opportunity to serve when, at Brother Claude's prompting, they
helped soothe the distress of two visiting sisters, who
were sobbing after hearing his words.

Afterwards, the whole team was involved in
uplifiting conversation. Then, just as its members were
walking out of the house with Ambrosio and Priscilla, a
rowdy group—mocking and out of control—appeared
from out of the fog.

The group burst into curses, their words contemp-
tuous and obscene.

Claude turned to alert the two new recruits. "Don't
worry," he said. "Occurrences like this are pretty normal."

"Scoundrels! Go away! Get out of here!"

One of the assailants, who had an extremely loud
voice, yelled at them, "We don't want your sermons or
your advice."

In return, Claude, refusing to return this salvo of

insults, spoke in a powerful and calm voice, lacking any trace of anger. "Brothers! Those of you who want a new life with Jesus—consider us your friends from now on! Come to the true liberation! Join the Christ!"

"Hypocrites," thundered the same voice. A roar of ironic laughter from his companions went up in reply. "We don't want anything to do with Jesus! You're nothing but impostors. You're just like us, only dressed up in those old saints' robes. Hey, if you want freedom, get rid of your clay wings! Hah! Angels without wings! You're so decked out, but you're nothing but dogs! You're just as human as us! If you had the guts, you would stop acting like a lot of old fuddy-duddies, shake off your tired old rules, and be free as we are!"

After these words, the mob started advancing on the worshipers. It was then that Claude, evidently in prayer, raised his right hand.

To the astonishment of Ernest and Evelyn, a ray of light shone out, filling the small space between the two groups. The pitiful band stopped, horrified. Some of them fell to the ground, as if they had been traumatized by an irresistible force; others resisted, yelling insults; still others ran away.

Among the ones left standing was a young man who cried out in an unforgettable tone. "Evelyn! Evelyn! Is that you there? Ah! I'm alive, we're alive! I want Jesus! Lord! Help me! Help! I want Jesus!"

Claude, filled with compassion at this plea, nodded his head in the affirmative. He shouted, "Come on, then! Come on!"

The young man tore himself away from the gang and hurried to the spot Claude indicated.

Within a few minutes, Evelyn, trembling and disheartened, stood before Tulio Mancini, the young fellow she had loved in another time and whose fall into the darkness of suicide had been, she was convinced, her fault.

Chapter 14

NEW DIRECTIONS

C onfused, Evelyn could say nothing.

"Evelyn! Evelyn!" cried the young man, a manic elation ringing in his voice. "Now that I see you, I know I am alive. Alive!"

Listening to his outcry, Claude considered the sensitive nature of the situation and recommended that Tulio board at Ambrosio's home, at least until he had a chance to adapt to his new environment and hospitalization could be arranged. Claude then administered magnetic healing to calm the young man's emotions and took him to the couple's dwelling where they, kindly and in friendship, did their best to make him welcome.

Not long afterwards the relief team returned to its own familiar territory.

Claude, a perceptive psychologist, thought it better not to refer, at least in personal terms, to what had just happened. He did, however, briefly mention to Ernest and Evelyn that it would be possible for them, if they wanted, to visit Evelyn's reencountered friend the next day. He would, he promised, give them precise information about where Tulio would be staying, that is, as soon as he had met with the director in charge of relief work. He expected Tulio to be assigned to a convalescence unit.

For his part, Ernest wanted to hear all about Evelyn's impressions of this young suicide, whom she had mentioned so often in their conversations. Nonetheless, he kept quiet. Evelyn, as she walked beside him, her arm through his, had fallen into a deep silence.

She still seems greatly puzzled, he thought.

A welter of contradictory ideas sped through his mind, rousing more questions than answers. Wasn't Tulio a suicide? He had read a good deal of material on what happens to suicides after death, and believed that they suffered hard, self-imposed penalties for defying God's Laws. How was it then that Tulio Mancini had managed to escape the punishment he deserved? Why had he been wandering around free among idle and rebellious spirits in an area reserved for the mentally disturbed?

Ernest was too polite to impose on Evelyn with these questions. Instead he decided to soothe her in her perplexity. She, after all, deserved all his respect.

Little by little, the members of the team went their separate ways, wishing each other peace and exchanging handshakes and hugs. Once alone with Evelyn, Ernest, always the generous friend, tried to dispel the constraints that seemed to be hemming in her thoughts.

With a smile, he spoke to her in the most careful manner he could manage, hoping to instill in her some calm and optimism: "My dearest Evelyn, if there were ever any doubts in our minds about the death of our physical bodies, which have probably disintegrated and disappeared from Earth some time ago, we have to pack them away now."

Evelyn tried to smile in return, without success. She felt crushed, discouraged.

Ernest redoubled his efforts to help her regain some measure of self-control. He kept reassuring her, then finally brought the subject back to Tulio.

"Haven't we asked for work? Who knows? Maybe the authorities here led us to today's discovery without our knowing it. This Tulio you used to dream about— he might be the start of a new direction for us, a new occupation, a path of access to our spiritual ascent, which we have to put in motion. Anyway, he is obviously in need of help, isn't he? His voice sounds so tormented, and his eyes look so...sickly. We're faced here with someone who needs immediate attention, and to tell you the truth, since he is an acquaintance of yours, he's our close friend in a way. In fact, we are the only support he has now."

Earlier Evelyn had mentioned in passing that her discovery of Tulio had caused her pain and horror, so Ernest now came back to his initial bantering humor. He threw his arms open in a gesture of mock astonishment and joked, "What better thing would Evelyn want to start work on?" He put his hands on his waist, one of

his characteristic poses, and added, "Besides, my dear
Evelyn, as a philosophical old friend of mine once said,
'Be a friend, and be light'. We're discarnate now and we
need moral training more than ever. If Tulio's presence
calls us to work that will test our capacity to love our
neighbor, let's not fiddle around but get to it."

Several days went by before the two friends were
able to see the young man again. By then he had received treatment and looked considerably improved. At
the first meeting, Ernest studied him curiously. For her
part, Evelyn was both surprised and baffled. This was a
different Tulio Mancini from the one she remembered.
He stared at her with piercing eyes that seemed to give
away strange, disconcerting ideas. Right in front of them,
she and Ernest could see the dirty designs growing inside him, though he didn't have the slightest notion that
he was being so intimately seen and scrutinized.

Without consciously intending it, Ernest and Evelyn
began exchanging impressions telepathically. They realized for the first time how possible it was for them to
talk between themselves this way, spontaneously, as it
were, and how preferable this medium was, especially
in front of someone who didn't share their ideals and
emotions. At that moment, they were sure they were
reading Tulio's soul as if it were an open book. They
particularly felt the enthusiasm of the young man, who
imagined himself to be still alive in the physical world
since he had just met his former fiancée. It was an illusion they dare not suddenly destroy.

"What amazes me the most is that I put up with

this for so long, that I was so full of doubt," said Tulio, with a tone of relief..

Evelyn tried to change the direction of his thoughts, a tactic aimed at better preparing him for the truth. "As far as I am concerned," she said, in her friendly way, "the most hurtful thing was your attitude, shooting yourself like that. It was madness!"

"Shoot myself? Who me? Me! But don't you know?" He seemed amazed. "I never did that! It's true I was weak enough one day to think of poisoning myself because I thought I had lost you. But later I saw that you hadn't rejected me at all, and I wanted to do everything I could to win you back. What happened was that Caio, who was anxious to put me out of the running for you, came to see me. He asked to go to the office with me so we could go over a book on international law together. He claimed it was urgent, so I didn't hesitate. It was a holiday and the offices were empty. Once we were alone together, he dropped the pretense that we were there on business and started accusing me. He said I was a coward and that my poisoning myself was just a ploy to end the love between you and him. I tried to defend myself. I told him that my love for you was pure, honest. But he started bullying me, insulting me in ways I will never forget. Then he took out a revolver and shot me in the chest

"I fell to the floor. Everything went black. Sometime later, I woke up in a hospital room, and since then I have been sick and full of anger, but trying to get back my health so that I can take care of that scoundrel in the way he deserves."

If a lightning bolt had struck the three of them at that moment, it couldn't have destroyed Evelyn's confidence more completely than this revelation. Evelyn thought, 'Tulio didn't leave his body by suicide at all! He was killed by the man I married!'

The same realization simultaneously flashed through Ernest's mind; the young man had been the victim of an undetected crime!

Ernest sensed Tulio wanted to be alone with Evelyn but, perhaps out of a sense of guilt at leaving her, he begged telepathically that she not try to bring the young man to reality, but wait until they could formulate a plan to help him. Evelyn understood, and Ernest asked to be excused. He wanted to think, to relax. Besides, he told her, it was natural that the two of them might have things of a personal nature to say to each other, and he would meet with her later.

Evelyn was a little uneasy with this idea, but agreed.

When she turned back to Tulio, however, she felt slightly helpless, as if she were confronting hidden dangers. Tulio invited her to walk for a while in the park of the institution where he was staying.

A few minutes later they were strolling side by side among calm-inducing trees and flowery hedges, breathing in the sweet scent of the place. "Evelyn," Tulio began, "who is this old fellow you are hanging around with?"

Evelyn was painfully aware of the sarcasm in his voice. Nonetheless, she answered gently, "He is a very distinguished friend of mine. I owe him favors I can never repay."

"You have to understand," came the reply, "that I have suffered a lot trying to find you. So I don't want to lose your company to any other man again, even if he is your own father."

Evelyn was going to answer and ask him to be more reasonable but Tulio continued, excitedly: "Evelyn, there is a world of things I want to know, that I want to ask you and hear from you. I don't know if I have been hallucinating or what the situation is. I need to know where we are and what we are doing here. But first, I want to talk about you and me. Just us."

At this point in the conversation, they came across a lovely little gazebo hut, completely covered in bindweed. Tulio asked, a hint of pleading in his voice, if they could rest there for a while. It hurt him to move around too much, he said. Since being shot he hadn't felt the same. Feeling sorry for him, Evelyn agreed, and they went inside.

They sat down on one of the gazebo's many benches, and the young man looked around to make sure they were absolutely alone. Then he closed the door, so that the only light now coming in streamed from tall, narrow windows that reached almost to the ceiling.

Tulio turned to her with such an expression of passion on his face that she trembled.

"Evelyn! Evelyn," he said wildly, "You know I have been waiting and waiting for this moment through all of these terrible years! For us to be together again!"

In truth, Evelyn was not at all insensitive to this appeal. Tulio was, after all, a young man she had once loved, and he still had power over her. She remembered their evenings in the parks and movie theaters together, moments when they had whispered tender things to each other in the days before she had made a commitment to Caio. Yes! This was the same Tulio who had once so impressed her. The same affection, the same loving voice. It seemed to signal to her a renewal of her destiny. Instinctively, she remembered Caio's infidelities; the mockery of love dressed up in the beautiful words she had heard from him so many times. For a moment her heart was uncertain. Once again, as she had done during her engagement, she wavered between the two men. Now once again, Tulio was before her promising ardent, unbroken love. His words were enough to make her feel giddy with delight, but her conscience had grown too keen for her to give in completely. She caught herself and forced a readjustment in her thinking. A strange feeling, drawing her to him, seemed to dominate her; but there was something in Tulio at that instant that frightened, even repulsed her. He wasn't the gentleman he had been in the old days. He had become reckless, bitter. With this in mind, she struggled to restore her moral balance, telling herself she wasn't about to agree to any suggestion not in keeping with her integrity as a married woman. She owed loyalty and respect to her husband. Indeed, it was the notion of the vows she had made, no matter what they had meant to Caio, that saved her soul's nobility and sincerity right there and then. She was able to impose strength and serenity upon herself, and resolved to keep a rein over emotions that she realized, for the time being, were unreasonable.

While these thoughts raced through her mind, Tulio was saying, "Let me hold you, Evelyn, I want to feel the warmth of your heart. I need you! I am like a thirsty man who has just found an oasis in the desert. Please, have pity on me!"

He began to take her in his arms. Startled, she struggled in his embrace, trying to draw back. "Tulio, get hold of yourself," she demanded. "Don't you know that I married Caio and have the responsibility of a home?"

"Caio? That idiot? Well, I understand that my being away for so long must have driven you to marry him. But things aren't going to stay this way." He paused for a few seconds, then said to the frightened woman, "Evelyn, I know my feelings are still important to you! Come on! Give in, just a little."

He tried to kiss her. The attempt dismayed and frightened her. Somewhere—thank God—she found the strength to pull back from him. "Tulio," she said indignantly, "what are you doing? You are acting crazy!"

"Since the day I took the bullet from that rascal— and I'll put him in prison yet, Evelyn—I have thought about you day and night. There is no one else on my mind! Won't you have pity on me?"

His tone of voice hurt her deeply, but she said firmly, "I understand your feelings for me, and I am glad you remember me, but do you think it's right to attack me like this? Don't you see that it is insulting? I have told you already that I have a husband and have to be faithful."

Tulio was quiet for a moment.

Then his eyes glared. Disturbing thoughts took control of his mind. He reacted to her cry for understanding with sarcasm.

"A husband! A husband, that rake!" He laughed, his voice again full of mockery. "The people where I was, the people from the Land of Liberty, are absolutely right, I can see now. You are one of the saints. But I make no pretense of being anything more than what I am, a fully functional man. I desire you—does this shock you? What a laugh! You are a woman, no different from any other woman. You're no better than the ones I know in the Land of Liberty, except that you try to hide it in a cloak of self-control. A pretty tattered cloak, too."

"Yes," Evelyn murmured, hurt, "I won't deny that I am human and fragile. But don't you think that self-control is the best way for us to educate ourselves and refine our feelings and thoughts?"

"Hah!" Now, he laughed bitterly. " Obligation is a straight jacket that the hypocrites put on the simpletons. But you will change your mind."

In agony, Evelyn took refuge in silent prayer, asking for help from the powers on high. Meanwhile, Tulio moved toward her, a sneer on his face. "Look inside yourself and you will see what you are covering up," he said. "You're a lead-footed angel, Evelyn, like the other monkeys in fancy clothes around here. Stop acting that way! We are all free! Children of Nature, free to do as we please! Show some independence if you don't want to end up in the slave quarters of the hypocrites in power here!"

He came closer to her, ready to take her in his arms, when someone, providentially, knocked at the door.

Embarrassed, Tulio immediately recovered his composure and went to answer it.

The newcomer promptly announced his position and his assignment. He was an assistant to Instructor Rivas, he said, and had come with orders to take Sister Evelyn Serpa to the Institute of Spiritual Protection on a matter of some urgency.

Relieved, Evelyn took a deep breath. Her silent prayer had been answered. She thanked the messenger telepathically, and together the three spirits left, Tulio following the messenger closely. He then returned to the readjustment center, and once there was put in a segregated cell for further treatment.

Chapter 15

MOMENTS OF ANALYSIS

Ernest and Evelyn, who were anxious for an explanation of the facts surrounding Tulio's situation, asked for a meeting, which Instructor Rivas agreed to. Determined to take advantage of this kindness, the two friends arrived promptly.

In the Institute's secure atmosphere, Rivas listened to their questions patiently. Why was the young man so disturbed? What was the best way for both of them, especially Evelyn, to help? Would it be proper for them to ask the Institute for information concerning Tulio's accusations against Caio? Would they be able to assume the responsibility for helping him?

When they had finished, their adviser gazed at them gently. "You have requested spiritual work several times already," he said, "so don't be surprised if the time to begin has arrived." He paused briefly and smiled. "Tulio Mancini is the starting point for the redeeming work you have embraced. But first, look into your own

hearts, especially you, Evelyn, and be sure you understand the feelings his situation is causing in both of you.
Where love is in equilibrium, our conscience doesn't
bother us. Where there are no pains of conscience, there
is no guilt."

"Please, Instructor Rivas," Evelyn appealed, "tell me
all I have to do!"

"I will tell you exactly, as if you were my own children. Between parents and children there should be the
utmost sincerity."

Then changing his tone, he said, "Evelyn, what
were your feelings when you were alone with your
friend?"

Evelyn had secretly decided to tell the truth, no
matter what the consequences. "Well," she confessed,
"when we were together with nobody watching us I
seemed to be caught up in all my memories of the old
days, when I thought I had found in him the man of
my dreams. I felt young again, and then..."

The instructor, noting the reticence in her voice, finished the last difficult phrase for her: "And then your
own emotional vibrations encouraged his passion for
you."

"But then I suddenly remembered that I was married and brought my emotions under control."

"Good for you!" said Rivas. "But your heart still
spoke, provoking that scene of uncontrolled passion, a
condition Tulio first fell victim to on Earth—largely,
Evelyn, because of your unfulfilled promises to him."

"Oh Lord!"

"Now, don't let it upset you! Before the Divine Laws, we are all spirits in debt. We're also in a state of transition from narcissistic self-love to disinterested love. True, we have theories about the sanctity of our feelings, but in essence and in practice we are simple initiates. When it comes to elevated thoughts, we simply take in the overflow from Higher Planes. In the field of lower impulses though, we are still carrying the huge weight of instinctual desires, and these desires have a strong appeal to us on the lower planes."

Impressed, Ernest interjected, "You mean that humans on Earth . . ."

"Are beings whose intelligence has been refined by powers acquired on the evolutionary path they have treaded for many centuries. Yet, in general, they still go back and forth between their animal nature and their cultured character. On the other hand, there are others who have already advanced from the stage of humanity to angelhood. Most of us, who are still undergraduates from Earth's school, find ourselves, where sexual behavior is concerned, in transit from polygamy to monogamy. That is why we have to keep watch over ourselves, especially since we know that in the realms of body and soul, sex is a creative energy."

Rivas didn't want to move too far away from Evelyn's specific problem, so he broke off this interesting explanation and turned back to her.

"Evelyn, it's understandable that you felt and communicated that attraction, and you were very right to restrain yourself. The only way we can put a brake on our impulses is through clear and responsible thoughts. We're all looking for spontaneous self-respect as a port of arrival, but getting there requires traveling along the currents of life for a long, long time. What we do in those travels is learn to manage self-discipline. Where feelings are concerned, we have to learn to take the blame for our errors so that, when the right time arrives, we can heal or redeem them."

Evelyn, disheartened, sighed.

"Yes, I have to recognize that I owe a debt to Tulio" she said. "I made so many promises to him and then left them unfulfilled."

"That's right. So far Tulio has made a good many mistakes. But your own conscience is not about to let you out of your obligations in this matter."

"How can I pay my debt, then?"

"Help him cleanse his own emotions, just as someone might purify muddy well water." Evelyn's anxiety now became evident, and Rivas moved to calm her.

"But we can't go about this recklessly or through violence," he continued. "We have to accept ourselves as we are and face the problems our own errors have caused. We don't analyze ourselves to find reasons to cry. You are aware that you have been partially the cause of his moral downfall. Let's calmly see how we can get him back on the right track."

"I seem to have so little to offer," Evelyn said humbly. "What can I do?"

Rivas went over to a large piece of furniture, a complicated filing cabinet, and took out a file. In it, he explained, was summarized all the information Evelyn had provided during her first Institute interview. Along with this version of the events that had tormented her life on earth, he said, he had tried to find complementary information concerning her path. This is how he came to realize that Tulio had lost his physical body because of Caio Serpa who, in turn, had made Tulio's murder look like a suicide and was able to convince the police authorities that was what had happened. A perfect crime. Tulio, as a victim of premature death, wandered around in confusion for a while, staying close to where the tragedy had occurred. Finally, he was brought to this very place for treatment. He convalesced for a few months, but the passion Evelyn had inadvertently stirred up in him caused him to fix his thoughts on and around her. This being the case, he missed a chance for spiritual improvement. Eventually he ran away to the same shadowy region where he was found. He had spent the last few years there, self-exiled, doing all kinds of foolish things. He was bound to Evelyn, who stirred so many empty dreams of love and happiness in him, and this caused him to degenerate and lose all self-respect. Now, he has come back here, to this oasis of healing and restoration, only because he has once again met the woman his heart couldn't forget. Consequently, this is now his new chance for self-reeducation."

Evelyn and Ernest listened with astonishment to this exposition, delivered with such incontestable logic. To Evelyn's painful questions about her future duties, Rivas answered, "Sister, we can tell you that, because of your undeniable merits, benefactors and friends of yours in the higher realms asked the agents of Divine Justice not to let you depart the physical life before beginning your spiritual rehabilitation on Earth. Remorseful, under the assumption that Tulio Mancini committed suicide, you attracted the suffering spirit of an actual suicide to you. Sentenced by his own conscience, the spirit you aborted went through the trials of a failed body in order to learn greater respect for the divine gift of physical life. It's easy to see, then, how the grief you felt at not becoming a mother was extremely useful to you on Earth, since it has given you the chance to make precious reparation."

"Still, we have been told that he didn't die by his own hand, that he was murdered by a rival," Ernest said.

"In spite of that," Rivas replied, by way of correction, "let's not forget that, led on by Evelyn's actions, he had tried to take his life once before, and in so doing suggested Serpa's crime."

Then, noting their reaction, Rivas added with a kind smile, "We're friends here simply examining the law of cause and effect. Let's understand that justice works within us."

"But..." Ernest, surprised at this answer, started a half-hearted reply, then gave up. Faced with the calm of Rivas's rational explanation, he didn't know how to introduce new arguments.

Rivas once again took up the thread of his argument. "We are automatically drawn to persons and circumstances that are in tune with ourselves or our problems," he said. "Evelyn stirred suicidal thoughts in this man whose love she had gained, but then she switched from thoughtless action to repentance, consciously seeking to make amends as soon as she found out about his moral collapse. Only then, compelled by her conscience, did she become aware of how her actions had injured someone who had had complete confidence in her, and how she had hurt herself as a result. She came to regret what she had done to Tulio Mancini and at the same time to hate herself. While in this guilty state, she became a vessel for an entity under similar conditions to those which she supposed had driven Tulio, thus becoming pregnant with a suicide's soul anxious to atone for his own crime."

He gave Evelyn a friendly look and went on. "Unconsciously expressing the desire to atone for her acts, her intent reached the hearts of friends and benefactors in the Spiritual World. They advised, Evelyn, that you be granted this grace we spoke of before. This is how, eager as you were to free Tulio from the harm you had caused him before dying, you suffered the penalty you thought you deserved. You didn't pay him the debt directly, but rather by *helping* an anonymous suicide, a child of God as we all are, thus redeeming yourself inwardly in accordance with the laws that rule our conscience. The unknown brother who died suffered the trial of not being born, but he also started to pay off the debt he had contracted with himself. How? By learning the value of the real treasure that is the physical body, our tool for attaining perfection and progress."

Ernest and Evelyn listened with surprise to these remarks, but Rivas wasn't finished. "Eternal Justice is served in our inner consciousness. God doesn't condemn or absolve us. Universal Love is always ready to lift us up, to instruct us, to better us, to elevate and sanctify us. Our destiny is the sum of our own acts, and its results are exact. We always owe the situations we face in life to ourselves, we receive from life exactly what we put into it."

"Then, what now?" asked Evelyn, frightened.

"Circumstances, Evelyn, have brought your creditor to you because fortunately you are now in a position to carry forward the work of his rehabilitation."

"What shall I do?"

"If you're truly ready to start on this path again, now is the time to help Tulio get rid of the sick ideas your behavior as a capricious young woman put into his head. Become his devoted guardian from now on, get him ready to transform his vision of life in the spiritual plane."

"I can't be a wife to him."

Like a father, Rivas took her hands in his. "If a woman's errors were not committed as a partner in a man's sexual life, she doesn't have to become his wife just because she owes him some other debt. The same holds true in regards to a man. But despite this principle, the law of love has to be applied, no matter what form of expression love takes." Then, in a tone of the deepest kindness, he said, "You can restore Tulio's emotional field right here and purify your own feelings toward him simultaneously. Support and instruct him as a mentor, but a motherly one. Almost always, an individual's recuperation is like a sublime fruit of the soul; it only ripens because someone else's self-denial has nourished it through the protection of love and the dew of tears."

With these words, Evelyn was left bathed in hope and Ernest in deep meditation about eternal truths.

Needed elsewhere, Rivas was pressed for time, but before going he promised to continue their conversation as soon as a new opportunity arose.

Chapter 16

REVITALIZING WORK

A new life now started for Evelyn and Ernest, but more especially for Evelyn. Helping Tulio, encouraging him, guiding the renewal of his ideas, became pressing tasks. In order to accomplish it all, the two friends enrolled in courses focusing on the sciences of the spirit. Soon, they were radiant with hope and enthusiasm. The courses offered an opportunity to examine topics such as Gospel fundamentals, self-transformation, mental forces, feelings and emotions, violent behavior, self-control, spiritual influences, and reincarnation.

In order to talk constructively to the young man, Evelyn took courses on how to improve logical reasoning. To her had fallen the most serious task: undoing the tangled thread of illusions she had helped create in his mind. For his part, Ernest, who pitied Tulio greatly, could, on instruction of the Institute of Protection, only accompany her from a distance. To him was given the duty of intervention, should it become necessary.

The day finally arrived when their work was to begin. They were to see Tulio three times a week, their tasks being divided into two parts: visits for explanation and visits for nursing. On the first day, Rivas personally went with them to the mental health ward where their new duties were to be carried out. There he introduced them to the directors and staff of the readjustment center and with the general approval and good will of all those individuals, they set off to work.

In this small community of ailing souls, Tulio was a recluse. He lived in an isolated room which, Rivas said, was built of a special material that filtered out those vibrations likely to reconnect him with his earlier, undesirable company. The young man welcomed Evelyn with delight and in the beginning spent a considerable time reassuring her of his vows of love in tones of loyalty and tenderness.

In response, Evelyn redoubled her cautions. She framed these in terms of endearment, even as she prayed for inspiration. The therapeutic sessions went on regularly, but Tulio remained fixated on her. At times, he reminded her of a boat moored to a marina, incapable of leaving port.

No sooner would she create the right atmosphere for the lessons than he would begin complaining like a sick child. He was feeling under the weather, he would say, and unable to think clearly, or he would claim that he felt diminished and neglected. Nor did he have any need for the philosophical considerations she kept bringing up. And he had no inclination whatsoever toward matters of faith. He was, he insisted, simply a *man-man*, in his own definition. In such a condition, it was clear, he didn't want a nurse or a teacher, even one as solicitous as Evelyn. What he wanted was a mate, the woman of his dreams.

Evelyn listened patiently to these outbursts and complaints and as best she could, she warded off his emotional blows and pruned his destructive thoughts, helped always by Ernest, who kept watch over all her activities and did whatever he could for her. Her new responsibilities now took up most of her time, and since she recognized her own deeply emotional nature, she concentrated constantly on Caio, investing in him her entire potential for affection. If she were to be a motherly mentor to Tulio, as Rivas had advised, she would need to feel like Caio's wife all the more. Thus, at every step she visualized his image, silently sending him her most beautiful thoughts. True, Caio had not been an ideal husband; and she knew now that he was a murderer—one , moreover, with the cunning to hide the fact. Yet being a human being like any other he'd become a criminal out of love for her. He had eliminated Tulio as a rival for her affections—not coldly, but in a fit of passion. She longed to see him again in person, to feel the warmth of his presence, and to energize herself for the moral battles she was engaged in. But, no matter how often she and Ernest requested permission to visit their earthly families, they regularly received the same answer from their own mentors, "Too early." As a consequence, they took comfort in study and work.

Once in a while, in a *tête-à-tête*, they shared confidences. Ernest would speak tenderly of his wife Elyse and his daughter Celine. He would weave on the magical loom of his memory images of them both as crystal mirrors of love into which he looked, delightfully, to find his own reflection, even though his daughter sometimes had rebelled against him and treated him cruelly. At least he could be sure that neither Elyse nor the girl were going through financial hardships: he had left them a large income and a good house. He had also put some money in safe investments that would provide them with a solid pension. Then there was also the insurance he had secured for them.

But—still there was the absence. Ernest questioned himself constantly, turning to Evelyn, who had become almost like a sister.

Yes, he thought, *still the absence, and the distance!*

At times, the two friends would lose themselves in daydreams, anticipating their happiness in meeting their loved ones again. By now they knew enough to realize that between themselves and their families on Earth there was a *wall of different vibrations*. In view of that, gaining their families' attention would be impossible— after all, it wasn't as if they were simply coming back from a long trip! So for now, as far as transformations were concerned, they had no choice but to conform to their mentors' wishes. Moreover, they had heard all kinds of stories from the *dead* who had returned from Earth—had, in fact, listened to their tales of discouragement and sadness because relatives hadn't been able to see, hear, touch, or even notice them. Some, it's true, came back consoled and hopeful, as if freed from ties that weighed heavily on their hearts. Many others, though, were disenchanted, moody, and little inclined to talk. When they did refer to family and friends, they spoke mostly of radical changes in feeling and attitude.

Nonetheless, both Evelyn and Ernest remained optimistic and trusting. Evelyn grew more enthusiastic every day, and in the company of the attentive Ernest, only the most positive thoughts flowed from her lips. Caio, in her opinion, may have been guilty of small peccadilloes; but he had rehabilitated himself, according to her ideas of a good husband, by the tenderness and self-denial he had shown during her final illness. It was true that he might have been unfaithful for a while: he was a man governed by his physical appetites, and he was obviously having his fun as he waited for her to recover. But once confronted with her death and imminent departure, he had changed, seeming to recapture the love and tenderness she had known in him as a fiancé. In her mind's eye, Evelyn saw him suffering and unhappy, anxious to be free of the flesh, and to take her in his arms again. As Ernest listened with interest to all these sweet expectations, she tried to fend off any objections he might raise. Notwithstanding Caio's actions, she asserted, he had even been mad enough to eliminate Tulio in order to marry her, a terrible calamity to be sure. Resolutely she declared that in the same way that she was working for Tulio's rehabilitation now, she would later

on exert herself for Caio, doing her best to help him make
the necessary reparations. Still, behind this thought she
knew lay vanity, at least in part. More than anything
else she wanted to be wanted.

Ernest would then start retelling his life-story,
dwelling especially on his home life. He loved his wife
deeply and confessed he had made many blunders
when he was younger, all in order to keep domestic
peace. His daughter, Vera Celine, the gift that had
warmed his heart throughout his married life, was in
these idylls always tender, understanding, devoted. He
had dreamed of a good and caring husband for her; but
he had left her, at age twenty-two, with no marriage
prospects in sight. It pained him, as it would any father
so far away from home. But he had the greatest confidence in her. Her future didn't worry him. Why, even
with her appreciable allowance, she was also teaching
English, which she did masterfully. She was earning
money, and she knew how to save.

Thus, the two friends held long and frequent conversations together, always thinking nostalgically of the
past and celebrating it.

After six months of Evelyn attending to and in-
structing Tulio, Rivas came to look at him personally.
He called for the charts, kept by the head of staff, to
verify Evelyn's punctuality and efficiency. Then, assuming his role as a doctor, he entered the patient's room to
give him a thorough examination. As soon as he saw
Tulio, he realized how little the young man had ben-
efited from his two mentors' lessons. Indifferent, Tulio

held fast to one central idea: Evelyn. With her as the center of his thinking, his ideas swirled around her: the need to possess her for himself, Caio's murder of him, his desire for revenge, his dark illusions of self-pity. His heart was heavy with suffering, and Rivas couldn't find the slightest gap through which a ray of hope and optimism might filter.

To Rivas's question about how he felt, Tulio answered with the sadness of the patient who knows no cure is possible: "Well, doctor, without Evelyn next to me, I can't understand anything. If she reads me the Gospel, I think that she and only she is the angel who can save me. If I consider her teachings about self-control, I see her in my mind as the only lever strong enough to govern me. If she encourages me to have faith, I end up wanting her all to myself. If she explains something about spiritual disturbances I finish the lesson admitting to myself that, if I could, I would leave this hospital to run after and hold her in my arms, even if I had to go to the ends of the earth."

Rivas smiled in his fatherly way, and counseled calmness and steadiness. "Let's think carefully, son. We're eternal spirits. You have to maintain your serenity, your patience. You can achieve happiness, with God's blessing, but it takes time."

The young man's reply was acid, irreverent; he neither asked for nor needed advice.

Rivas, who was a shrewd psychologist, took his departure.

That evening he went to visit Evelyn and Ernest.

He praised Evelyn's work of reeducation. It had been done with confidence. Tulio, however, hadn't reacted positively. He had lost all will power, and to his own detriment, had enclosed himself in fantasies. Rivas finished by telling Ernest and Evelyn, who had listened to him carefully, "I don't see any advantage in Tulio's remaining here. All we can do now is to get him to accept the constrictive operation[10] voluntarily."

"For a rebirth?" asked Evelyn, frightened. "Do we have to go that far?"

"Our friend is mentally ill," Rivas returned. "He's profoundly sick, traumatized, anguished, fixated. The only remedy is to start all over again. Unfortunately, on the road ahead he will find many difficulties and much turmoil."

Rivas didn't offer them further counseling, or other suggestions.

Both Ernest and Evelyn, absorbed in pondering the requirements and trials of reincarnation, grew suddenly silent, and Rivas left them alone to think their own thoughts.

---

[10] *Translator's Note: The constrictive operation is a preparatory process for reincarnation. The spiritual body undergoes a transformation of its essential structure in order to adapt to the denser conditions of the flesh. The process is explained in greater scientific detail in A. Luiz's* Missionarios da Luz, *1945, FEB, Brazil, chapter 13. For a more elaborate discussion on the spiritual body and reincarnation, see Allan Kardec's* The Spirits' Book, *1996, AKES, Philadelphia, chapters 5 and 11. The concept of spiritual body as considered here is similar to the one presented by Paul, "If there is a natural body, there is also a spiritual body." (1 Corinthians 15:44)*

Chapter 17

MATTERS OF THE HEART

Ten months had gone by since Evelyn and Ernest started their work with Tulio. One day the two asked for a meeting with Instructor Rivas. On the agenda were several problems that had constantly plagued them. Above all, they wanted to see their relatives on the physical plane again. Ernest had become a well of memories about his wife and daughter; and Evelyn could no longer stand the longing she felt for her husband and parents. They wanted desperately to return home, and thirsted for information and explanations with similar desperation.

The instructor, greeting them with his usual friendliness, agreed to recommend them for permits, then pointed out in his simple manner, "I believe both of you are ready for this venture. You've worked conscientiously, you've learned about many important subjects, and you understand the issues of reincarnation, the need for self-control, and the importance of personal change."

And with much tenderness in his voice, he added, "Any particular reason—something more personal—for this petition?"

In her shy way, Evelyn volunteered, "Instructor, I miss Caio so badly."

"Husbands and wives who love each other," interrupted Ernest, "start feeling as if they're engaged again when they're apart for very long. I have to confess that I'd love to throw my arms around my wife again."

"Dear friend," ventured Evelyn. She gave her mentor a significant look. "Talking about marital relations, I'd like to consult you about something."

"Tell me, Evelyn."

"You know, in my first meeting with Tulio, I felt for a few moments like the flighty young woman I used to be. I felt strongly attracted to him. Later I responded to that attraction by going back mentally to Caio's world— the physical plane—and I got the impression, from that experience, that I'm no more than a satellite, spinning around one man and then the other. As I started trying to help Tulio, little by little, I came to realize that he's absolutely not the man I want for a mate. To keep helping him and putting up with him I need some motivation."

"The love of God."

"I understand today we breathe the very essence of God. But—that's where the mystery lies for me. I know we can't accomplish anything without God; but, between God and my duties, I need someone to lean on, someone who'll be my support in daily life and the

search for the state of mind we call inner peace, euphoria, happiness. It's a spiritual hunger and it makes me
think day and night of seeing Caio again. Does it mean
that my husband is really my absolute love? Is he the
spirit who'll be my soul mate, the one I'll be with forever when we reach perfection?"

Rivas smiled. "We're all destined for Eternal Love,"
he said, falling into his philosophical mode. "However,
in reaching that supreme goal, each of us follows our
own path. For most of us, finding an ideal love is like
panning for gold. We have to sift out the gravel and dig
in the mud with our hands to get at it. Whenever we
love someone deeply, we transform that person into the
mirror of our own dreams. We start seeing ourselves in
the object of our affections. Now, if this person really
does reflect our soul, the love between us grows stronger and stronger. It provides us with a climate of encouragement and happiness on the voyage of evolution, which isn't always easy. In this way of thinking,
we have a secure support in our moral ascent. But if
that person is wrong for us, he or she ends up like a
bank that is incapable of properly managing our investments. That's when the spiritual perspectives we call
grief, disenchantment, indifference, and disillusion come
into play."

"You're saying, then, that we travel through our existence on paths of affinity," said Ernest. "We form attachment after attachment as we go along, until at last
we find one unforgettable being who touches our inner
lives with eternal love."

"That's right, but we can't think of this affection within the narrow confines of sex. Marriage is a sublime connection between individuals, but it's only one manifestation of love. Someone can realize the presence of his or her ideal type in a wife or husband, and yet, after the marriage, he or she may continue to be more closely attached to the heart of a mother or father. And sometimes they'll only find real affection in one of their children. In love, affinity is what counts."

Deeply impressed, Evelyn asked, "And what about unhappy marriages?"

"Reincarnation is also recapitulation," answered the instructor. "Many couples in the world are spirits who've come together again to accomplish specific tasks. In the beginning, their feelings are alike in the matter of affinity; they're like the cogs of two wheels—they complement each other so that the engine of marriage can work. Later on, they notice they have to improve parts of this living machine so that it produces the desired benefits. This requires understanding, mutual respect, constant work, and a spirit of sacrifice. If one or both partners distrust each other, the work started—or restarted—comes to an end."

"Then what happens?" Evelyn's question hung in the air. She was all curiosity now.

"Then, the mate who spoiled the adjustment—or both, depending on what caused the problem—has to wait for a new opportunity to rebuild the love they allowed to run down."

"May I ask another question, Instructor Rivas?

When the marriage of two persons who love each other is interrupted by physical death, can it be resumed over here?"

"Certainly, if you and your spouse really love each other, " said Rivas.

Ernest broke in, "And when that doesn't happen?"

"The one whose love is real continues to work, *on this side of life*, for the one on Earth who doesn't have the same level of feeling. This allows the work of love to be perfected in other ways—that is, apart from the affection between husband and wife."

Evelyn's face shone with a beautiful smile. "That won't happen to me," she said, sure of herself. "I have reasons today to trust Caio as much as I do myself."

"Your faith is a portrait of your sincerity," said the instructor.

Ernest glanced at his friend for a moment, admiring the tenderness of her good and frank spirit. He had been nurturing a deep tenderness for her for some time now. He had never caught her in an impropriety; she was always compassionate and unselfish. Many times he was surprised to find himself enchanted by her. What exactly was the lens through which his esteem for her manifested itself? Did he see her as a daughter, a companion, a mother, a sister? He couldn't say.

He was wary at the moment of getting caught up in such a digression. He decided to change the direction of these thoughts and brought them to an abrupt halt. "Instructor Rivas," he said, "just like Evelyn here, I'm convinced that my wife is waiting for me. But what if that doesn't happen?"

"If it doesn't happen," said Rivas, stressing the words with fatherly good humor, "you, Ernest, will no doubt enjoy helping her as a devoted friend."

"And do I have the right to choose a new wife in this new life?"

"Human laws, both on Earth and here, can be changed without essentially affecting Divine Laws. On Earth, no one, unless he or she wants to, has to be a widow or widower and go without companionship in a home. When the body dies, the duties of marriage die with it, and a man or woman can stay single if they want. The same happens here. A disincarnate man or woman can stay single or not, depending on his or her inner goals—but with this understanding—that they have in any situation the spiritual resources to honor the work of building the pure love that will finally end up guiding all our relationships."

Evelyn looked worried, and pressed for more knowledge. "Instructor Rivas," she said," do you have spirit friends who haven't been able to marry over here?"

"Yes, I'm one of them myself."

"Any special reason?" Ernest was curious at this answer.

"It just so happens that marital love, when expressed as pure love, continues to vibrate in harmony between the two worlds, with no interruption in the energy exchange between husband and wife. My wife and I were extremely close. On Earth, we were happy together; we fed each other the food of love. After disincarnating, I quickly noticed that our mutual bond went on as it always had, as if we were an integral part of a force field. Her spirit is dedicated to mine, and through that dedication I have a way to continue my apprenticeship in loving everyone. The same is true for her."

"An ideal union," exclaimed the delighted Evelyn.

Giving away her anxiety in trying to merge her love with that of her distant husband, she said, politely, "Instructor Rivas, I've noticed that whenever someone here mentions the possible passing of a loved one, our more experienced friends always become reserved. Sometimes I think it's a forbidden topic for us. Is that so?"

"Not really," replied Rivas. "As our sense of responsibility develops, we come to understand reincarnation as a school session. Each life is supervised by higher considerations that many times are hidden from us."

"Let's suppose I find my husband experiencing longings like mine, tormented and sad," said Evelyn, now betraying her own deepest desires. "Would it be possible to encourage him, even a little, with the thought that we would be happier over here, to promise him that we can try again after death? You know, I didn't leave him any children to help him through his suffering, to wait—"

"Evelyn, stop thinking like that," Rivas interrupted. "We don't have instruments to measure the faithfulness of our loved ones, and, even if your husband is tormented and having tremendous problems because of your absence, we don't know if dying would be the right answer for him. Maybe staying in the physical body longer is more desirable for him; he might need to become more secure as he matures spiritually. To put ideas of death into his head would probably help reduce the time he spends in his material experience. And who's to say that he'd be happy to return to the spirit life if we impose it on him rather than wait for nature? Nature is always wiser, because it reflects the designs of the Eternal."

"Oh, Lord!" Evelyn heaved a sigh. "How can I help him? His heart beats in me, Instructor."

"Very often when we say that someone's heart beats in ours," replied Rivas gently, "it would be wise to find out if our heart is beating in this someone, too." Then, in an even kinder tone, he added, "In a few days, you and Ernest will be able to visit your homes on Earth."

Overjoyed at this news, Evelyn and her friend thanked their mentor.

Suddenly, a sweet happiness took over their souls, as if their feelings had shifted away from a hazy melancholy and toward a shining sun of hope in a new dawn.

Chapter 18

THE RETURN

F inally, the day came when Evelyn and Ernest were to go home. They were as excited as kids at a party. Home, for the first time in two years!

At their departure, just before joining a small group of fellow travelers, who were returning to Earth under circumstances much like their own, Rivas told them, "You represent our city, our way of life, our principles. Behave on the basis of this new understanding. If you need help, call us through the mental wire." So saying, he hugged them both and wished them well.

The craft let them off near Via Anchieta[11] at the point where it divides, one road leading to São Bernardo.[12] There the small group dispersed, each member full of enthusiasm, each a living world of memory. The group leader set the return for the next day. The travelers were

---

[11] *Author's Note: Highway between the cities of Santos and São Paulo, in the state of São Paulo.*

[12] *Translator's note: A suburb of the city of São Paulo.*

to meet, at the same place, twenty hours later.

Amazed, Evelyn and Ernest breathed in the soft breeze. Hard to believe they were about to enter São Paulo! Entranced, they again saw the clear, intensely blue sky of a late May afternoon. Around them, gusts of cool air brought memories of old times. They walked together, fascinated, jubilant at heart. Yes, this was their old familiar city, the land they loved. Eagerly they inhaled the aroma of flowers and smiled at the travelers who, on this waning Saturday, were headed down to Santos.[13]

Evelyn, whose mind and heart were fixed on Caio's image, stopped once and gazed at Ernest as if looking into a full-length mirror. Tenderly, a little naïvely, she asked his opinion as a man on how she looked. She wanted to show the same simplicity and good taste, she said, that Caio liked to see in her at home. Oh, she knew very well the situation had changed. Caio wouldn't be aware of her presence as she would be of his. Still, she had heard that people who long for each other can sometimes see their loved ones with the soul's eyes—almost as if they were carrying around a TV receiver in their minds. If Caio concentrated his thoughts and feelings on her he would, surely, respond to her kisses, even if they weren't anything more than a vague memory by now.

---

[13] *Translator's Note: Santos - A resort city on the south coast of Brazil, about sixty miles from São Paulo.*

Ernest laughed as he listened and complimented her on her astuteness. He inspected her hair and face, advised her to make one or two minor adjustments to her dress, approved of her shoes—very much like a father appraising his daughter's looks on prom night. Afterwards he said jokingly that it didn't seem right for a young woman to go around looking so seductive. Evelyn defended herself—if anyone knew what her husband liked, she was that person!

In easy conversation, they were already walking through the district of Ipiranga,[14] where Evelyn hoped to find her husband in the same house where they had once been happy together. Suddenly, her happiness changed to uneasiness. As she drew closer to the old place, a sense of distress overtook her, the bliss of a moment ago merged with an unexpected anxiety. *What if Caio weren't at her own level*, she thought, *still loving and loyal?* Doubt tore at her spirit like a dagger twisting in her stomach.

"Ernest, do you have any feelings about what we'll find? Can you believe it—I'm feeling afraid right now? My knees are shaking."

"It's just a case of nerves."

"And is that all?"

Ernest gave her a deep and serious look. "Evelyn, do you remember the lessons we taught Tulio?"

---

[14] *Translator's Note: A district of São Paulo. It lodges the Ipiranga Museum of History.*

"Sure. But what does that have to do with us here?"

"Think about it. For months and months we've talked to Tulio, you especially, about matters of the soul: self-denial, understanding, serenity, patience. We reviewed and reviewed those lessons, going over the conclusions again and again."

"Yes."

"Don't you think that Instructor Rivas was doing the same thing for us with all his explanations about love and marriage, service and spirituality? Don't you suspect that our devoted friend was trying to teach us to look a little further down the road?"

"That's right, yes. I suppose so."

"So, let's prepare ourselves for some changes."

Evelyn pretended she hadn't understood this last remark and changed the subject. She was apprehensive, she said, and a little tired. She would like to rest awhile, if that was possible, since she didn't want to get anywhere near her husband feeling, or showing, any sign of upset.

Ernest suggested they rest for a few minutes in the museum gardens, so they headed in that direction, and soon found themselves relaxing at the foot of a water fountain. For a time, the waters calmed their thoughts.

Suddenly, as if he had caught a case of Evelyn's worries, Ernest fell quiet. At the very moment he was getting close to his wife and daughter, the initial enthusiasm of the trip started to wear off for him. He became lost in thought, and Evelyn, who couldn't help noticing the silence, started talking about happiness and hope, and how they should both be thinking positively. Ernest listened and took in her expressions of confidence, but they were only words. Evelyn felt frustrated. She'd become Ernest's sister and friend, but here, all at once, she found herself unable to penetrate the taciturn mood that had possessed him, so she stopped talking and declared, discreetly, that she was finally ready to start the final leg of the trip.

Always the gentleman, Ernest promised to help in her first contact with home. If everything went as expected, she would come back—he would be waiting nearby for a sign from her. He would then leave her with her husband until the next day, and go on to Vila Mariana,[15] where he hoped to see his own family. Evelyn agreed. She disliked being alone and didn't want to chance being without Ernest's support.

It was now six o'clock in the afternoon. Evelyn was no longer aware of São Paulo's sky, the rows of houses, or the passersby. Her heart pounding, she neared her old house. Reaching it, she crossed the patio and touched the door, which softly opened for her. Something told her Caio was at home. She went in, trembling and frightened, and inspected the room around her. It was still basically the same, with a few changes here and there in the furniture. To one side was her husband's narrow office, half visible through the open curtains. She entered it slowly, like someone going with

---

[15] *Translator's note. A district of the city of São Paulo.*

measured steps into a sanctuary. Books, papers and desk were all in order. Then, she noticed, leaning against a small flower vase, the photo of a woman. She searched the walls, looking for pictures of herself, for mementos of their past, but saw nothing. In a moment her thoughts turned pessimistic; the power of reason seemed to be extinguished in her. Most certainly, she thought, she had been replaced. Inwardly she raged, ready to explode in a storm of tears, but then caught herself, repeating the words of Rivas: "Behave on the basis of your new understanding." Upset, she walked further back into the house. Near the dining room in the small winter garden she had created, she came across a scene which she could not have prepared herself for; Caio was sitting with the young woman she had just seen in the photo.

He held the woman's right hand between both of his, slowly caressing it. It was a gesture of affection Evelyn knew well.

Revulsion and sadness mixed in her. She stepped back, away from the scene. Coldness crept into the fibers of her soul. She felt like fainting, almost as if she were dying again. She wanted to run into the room and reveal herself to them. At the same time, she longed to shout out and run away, to hide her face, and her immense pain, on Ernest's chest.

Instead, she sat down in a nearby chair, invisible to the two sweethearts, and tried to calm down.

A series of troubling questions rose in her mind. Who was this unknown woman? Was she the same one who had tormented her with those little notes to Caio, the ones covered with lipstick kisses? During her last days at home Caio had promised eternal love. Why then was he breaking that promise, knowing how much it meant to her? What kind of ties had he established here? Was he married or playing with the woman's affections, and so toying with life itself? In either case, what did the future hold for her?

She gazed at the two, astonished by their indifference to her. For the first time since her liberation, she realized how very narrow were the limits of the physical senses. Caio and his friend looked straight through her, many times, without seeing her. On the other hand, as long as she didn't leave, she had no choice but to see and hear them, just as if she were alive. She wanted to leave, to go away, but her emotions kept her glued to the spot.

Her soul ached. Her husband gave this new woman the same loving looks he had once given her. And there was more. She recognized a string of pearls, Caio's engagement present to her, around her rival's neck. Devastated, she started crying.

Her thoughts were ablaze now. But the teachings she had received had become part of her, and she could no longer ignore the subtle claims they held on her. For that very reason, she felt as if she was being tested, through this experience, on the progress she had made in her lessons with Rivas and her other friends from the Greater Life. She remembered Tulio. So many times she had taught him to detach from his emotions. Now, she saw, her own egotism and lack of resignation might be worse than his. She sought refuge in prayer, promising to do her best to be humble. She fought against herself, concluding that Caio was right in trying to be happy in any way he could. Little by little, she somehow managed to calm herself, and to pay more attention to the exchange going on in front of her.

"You, Vera," Caio was saying, with a smile, "have found in me a peaceful, sincere man. You ought to be proud."

"Then how do you explain that woman in your office?"

"Now, don't be so jealous. You know I'm a lawyer. I can't turn away clients. I'm an advocate of the people— I can't put myself out of their reach."

"In other words, I don't have any say in our relationship."

"Who told you that?"

"The phone call I got from that tramp the other day left me totally crushed. The things she told me about you!"

"Vera, if we paid attention to everything people said about us, life wouldn't be worth living."

"I just can't stand it anymore."

"Oh, come on! Can't stand what?"

The young woman Caio called Vera started crying. He brought her closer to him, and before Evelyn's startled eyes, kissed her a few times on the face and whispered, "Silly Vera! Happiness isn't a flower you can water with tears. Cheer up! I'm yours and you're mine. Isn't that enough?"

"At least if we were married—if I could use your name!—I'd know how to deal with these women that pester us."

"Darling, you're being absurd! You're exaggerating—you always do. I've told you I'll marry you, and I'm a man of my word."

"I've been waiting an awfully long time, it seems to me."

"And haven't I been waiting for you to settle things at home? Surely you don't expect me to live with a crazy mother-in-law the rest of my life!"

"Mother is so miserable; we can't just abandon her."

"I told you already, put the old hag in a home. She's already enjoyed her life; now it's our turn. Today we'll go to Guarujá[16] and look into this."

In reply, the young woman started sobbing. Caio stroked her hair, trying to console her. Evelyn, meanwhile, had regained her strength, and dragged herself out of the house. She longed for Ernest's presence, anxious to be back at his side. It was impossible to stay inside that house, the home she knew she had lost forever.

All her composure was now gone. The emotional disturbance had been too much for her. She called out loud for Ernest as soon as she found herself in the street. He appeared before her, and like a troubled child she threw herself into his arms.

---

[16] *Translator's Note: Guarujá - A posh beach in the Santos region.*

"Oh! Ernest, Ernest! I can't stand this any more!"

Together they backtracked part of the way, and he gently led her to a bench on the patio. Then, sitting next to her, he listened to her account of what had happened. Feeling ashamed, she told her story through smothered sobs, and Ernest, trying to forget his own fears, lost them in pity for her. He couldn't understand this tenderness that drove him irresistibly toward her. But these shared times, which always seemed to revolve around the most serious matters of the soul, had turned him into an unconditional friend. Listening to her, he shared her pain, rallied to her side of the story without a thought that it could have been any other way. Moved, he tried hard to calm her down.

"It's only fair that it's like this, Evelyn," he said, playing the part of adviser. "Caio is young. You and he weren't an old couple like Elyse and me. I think he has a place in his heart especially for you, but he has needs like any other man."

"But the young woman with him is the same Vera who used to write him those little notes I told you about. She's the same one! He was unfaithful to me before our separation, and he's unfaithful now. This proves it."

Ernest, like a father, patted her head and said, "I've been thinking and thinking. Don't you suppose that death has given us our true selves, and God has given us unselfish protectors, who have supported and instructed us so we could face the truth we're living today? What can we make of our earthly lives but a course in egotism or an apprenticeship in self-denial?" Ernest's pain showed in his voice. "Did we have husbands and wives to love, or to use as objects of pleasure, convenience, advancement in the world—mere objects? We talk so much about devotion when we're tied to our earthly bodies. But wouldn't the best time to prove the sincerity of our vows be after death? Couldn't this be the time when Caio most needs your consideration and tenderness?"

It wasn't so much his words as the way he said them that elicited in Evelyn a sense of compassion. In her mind's eye, she also started judging her husband from a new perspective. Caio was a young man, and God's designs had kept him tied to his physical body. How could she demand that he remain faithful to her and only her, in life and death, when he was still so far from understanding the importance of such constancy? She had been in the Spirit World for two years without even seeing him. How could she criticize his behavior? And this young woman, his girlfriend—why treat her as an enemy? Hadn't she seen the girl's tears, her suffering, in response to Caio's thoughtless, vacillating sarcasm? Couldn't she see herself in that girl's place, the victim of his half-hearted devotion, a sufferer from the distress he was causing?

Ernest went on these enlightening thoughts, and his words were both sensible and suggestive. "Remembering Rivas's lessons," he said, "I have to conclude that our instructors let you go on this trip so you would learn to forgive. And who knows, maybe this girl..." His voice dropped off suddenly.

"Maybe this girl what?" Evelyn asked, curious at the hesitation.

"Maybe this girl is the person in whom you'll be able to find a new mother for Tulio. We have studied some very complex subjects—passion and harmony, guilt and reincarnation—and our studies have led us to do a great deal of thinking. On the other hand, Rivas has also shown us what Tulio needs, without offering any real suggestions on how it can be achieved. But we know Tulio is relying on us during his readjustment. Think: he lost his physical body by way of Caio's bullet. Don't you think Caio will have to make up that experience to him—perhaps through the sacrifices and tenderness of a father? And what better chance than this one will you have to practice Jesus's teachings—loving someone you think of as an enemy and changing her into an instrument of help for the man you love, a man who's also in debt?"

She understood exactly how perceptive his comments were and, gratefully, fell into her friend's arms, sobbing and saying softly, "Oh! Ernest! Ernest!"

A few moments later a car backed out of the garage. Inside were Caio and Vera. Gaining control of herself, Evelyn told Ernest the two were going to Guarujá.

The young lawyer stopped the car momentarily and got out to close the garage door. For a second Ernest saw Caio's companion on the passenger's side.

At the sight of her, he turned pale.

More shocked perhaps than Evelyn had been, he stuttered, overwhelmed by anguish, "Evelyn, Evelyn, listen! This girl—this girl—is Vera Celine, my daughter!"

Chapter 19

LIFE'S REVISIONS

The two friends, stupefied, had no idea how to handle their overwhelming discovery. Ernest, disoriented, nonetheless remembered the beach house he had owned, and wasting no time, asked Evelyn if she would consider riding with him in the back seat of the car.

As they got in, bitter memories crowded into his mind. So this was the young woman Evelyn had mentioned so often! Vera Celine—his own daughter!

Tears streaked down Ernest's face. Evelyn, comforting him without words, held his hands in hers. She understood his pain as a father. He looked at her through his tears and said, "Do you know how much this hurts?"

"Calm down," whispered Evelyn gently, "we're more like brother and sister now than ever."

The car backed out into the street, and after a few minutes on the road, the front seat occupants started talking about details of the trip. In turn, each one began to reflect mentally the influence of the invisible passengers in the back.

Suddenly, as if by chance, Vera remembered Evelyn. "Caio," she said, "sometimes I ask myself if you're not in love with the memory of your wife. "

"Who? Me? That would be the last straw."

"Everybody tells me she was wonderful."

"She wasn't bad."

"And don't you miss her? Don't you feel her presence in your heart?"

Caio laughed mockingly. "Am I obliged to live with the dead, too?"

"I don't mean that. I'm talking about your natural grief—at losing her."

"Evelyn was dead for me a long time before her death certificate was signed. You know that."

"Lots of times I find myself looking at her portrait. Analyzing it. She had such a sweet look—and those big, sad eyes. It's impossible that you didn't marry for love!"

"Yes, I married for love. But love goes through stages, like everything else in life. First, it's all passion; then you lose interest."

"But why did you lose interest? Can you pinpoint the reason?"

"Do you want to know?"

"Yes."

"Well, I wanted very much to be a father. Evelyn was weak, sick. I believe it must have been something genetic. She got pregnant but then she had, on her physician's recommendation, to have a therapeutic abortion. Before that, I wasn't aware of these problems. But afterwards she became sick and disabled, and our marriage became a real hassle. During her last months, she prayed and cried all the time." He laughed openly. "The only thing I could do to stand it," he said, "was invent trips so I could come and spend time with you."

Evelyn held hard to Ernest, searching for support, for some way—after listening to such horrors—to cling to her honor.

Vera, not wanting to be disrespectful, changed the subject. "Caio," she asked, "we're going to have a house full of kids, aren't we?"

He quickly glanced up at her from the wheel. "It all depends," he said.

"On what?"

"Well, I know we're going to get married, Vera. But this business of raising kids isn't child's play. Are you prepared for it? Your mother's health isn't very encouraging, you know—all these spells, these attacks." Then, as if caught up in the thoughts being projected at him by the disincarnate man in the back seat, he added, "And what about your father?"

Her father, Vera knew, had died from a disease similar to Evelyn's, but, afraid to talk about it, she lied.

"He was pretty robust," she said. "Always healthy, always young. People used to think he was my brother."

"How did he die?"

"He had an operation—on a small skin tumor— nothing life-threatening, but he didn't take good care of himself afterwards. He wasn't completely well, but he started digging around in his garden. That's when he cut himself, and got an infection. It took his life."

"Tetanus?"

"That's right."

"What was he like mentally? Stable?"

"He was very intelligent, sometimes happy-go-lucky, like you. But he took life very seriously."

"I guess he had a very special affection for you—you being his only daughter and all."

"Not at all. Oh, he loved me all right. But all his time was taken up by his businesses—he managed several of them. He didn't have much time for home life. Of course, he made sure we didn't lack for money, so from the financial point of view, he was a good provider. But, as a father, I don't remember him ever listening to me or giving me advice about personal matters. When I was young and started having dates and getting involved with boys, I needed him very much, but—."

"He couldn't spare you an hour or two, eh?"

"That's what he used to tell me anyway. I could never tell him anything, even about my school problems."

Ernest listened, humiliated, disheartened. He would give anything to go back, to be the tender, attentive father he had failed to be. But there was nothing he could do.

The exchange between Caio and Vera went on.

"On the other hand, you certainly had your share of your mother's attention," Caio said.

"Wrong again," answered Vera. "I noticed very early in life that Mother was always moody and depressed. She liked being alone, and, even though she didn't neglect me exactly, I made most of the decisions about my life by myself. I'm still doing it."

"Did she and your father get along well?"

"Not at all. I think Mother put up with Father; she didn't actually love him. She tried hard to conceal it, naturally."

"Did the poor guy ever notice it?"

"I don't think so."

"So how do you explain the old lady's problems since he left? Not a reaction to losing him?"

"I doubt it. As soon as Father died, she underwent a big change for the worse. She had hated him behind his back, so she burned all the things he loved. She broke his watch, and tore up his photographs. Can you imagine that? She didn't even want prayers said for him, and she just became worse and worse. Eventually she got to where she is now and she refuses treatment. She isolates herself, talks to herself, laughs, cries, complains. Now she's threatening to close up the house and sit in the dark so she can see and hear the dead."

"Pretty weird," Caio concluded.

Despite Evelyn's sympathy, Ernest continued to cry during this conversation. His daughter's comments greatly surprised him. He felt as if he had hardly known her before this moment. It was true that, at home, he had been a man prone to emotional outbursts. But he had never had the slightest idea he was so

unnappreciated there. Could Celine be right? Why had
Elyse become so mentally unbalanced? What had really happened during his long absence?

The two spirits recognized that, in the course of
their introspection about these matters, both were undergoing a rigorous self-analysis.

Meanwhile, the car sped on. Finally, it slowed and
came to a stop. Their destination was a simple house,
softly lit in the enveloping night. Ernest was excited,
but cautious. As she had taken leave of him at Caio's,
he now left Evelyn in a spot nearby. He wanted to look
over the household situation by himself, he said. Later
on, he would decide whether it was a good idea to involve Evelyn in family conflicts. Besides, Vera's position—in the company of Caio—didn't encourage either
of them to go in together.

Evelyn agreed. She would use the occasion to pray
and meditate.

Touched by this kindness, Ernest entered his old
home. It was full of so many memories for him. In the
living room, everything was as he had left it. The table
and the carved chairs he had brought from the house in
Vila Mariana, along with the fishing gear, the armoire
with its old dishes, and the simple pictures hanging on
the walls—all was as he remembered it. He remembered,
too, the warmth of other times in the house, the good
times; and for all that he had lost, he cried. Not far from
the entrance he could see his daughter's room. She and
Caio were involved now in a lively conversation. Near
him, two steps away, he could almost touch the door to

the room where so many times he had lain next to his wife, the two of them breathing in the ocean breeze.

According to the clock, it was a few minutes past nine in the evening. *What would he find behind that closed door?* he asked himself restlessly. Elyse, sick? Disheartened? He recalled the lessons he had received from his friends in his new spiritual home: lessons that had strengthened him to face any surprises he might find in this earthly life. Still, he prayed to Divine Providence, asking for additional strength. He wanted to retain some measure of self-respect and dignity when he saw Elyse again. Vera's revelations in the car required that he be prudent, pay close attention to his own attitudes. After all, he wasn't there to complain, but to sing his gratitude for his loved ones, and give them what help he could. More than anything, he wanted opportunities to serve them.

With this attitude in mind, he passed through the door and found himself inside the bedroom. He knew it down to the most minute detail; nothing was out of place. Yet he could never have imagined the sight that greeted his eyes the moment he entered. Elyse was resting on the bed—her body thin, her face more deeply lined with wrinkles, her hair grayer, than he recalled. Right next to her, however, was lying someone else—a *disincarnate* man! Moreover, Ernest recognized him. It was the same man he had, so many years ago, shot in a jealous rage.

Ernest stopped, terrified. Instantly he thought of the last hunt he had taken part in, the trio of friends he had joined, the responsibility he had for the sorrow and suffering that had followed him the rest of his life. This man, the man lying there without a physical body, was his childhood friend, Dede, or rather the murdered man, Desiderio Santos, whose ghost he thought he had removed from his house.

Repentance came flooding over him; he grew numb with agony.

How was he supposed to deal with this enemy who was wounding him now in his nuptial bed?

Crying inwardly, Ernest nearly collapsed in despair. He realized now what powerful reasons Rivas had had for delaying this return. Just a few hours ago, he had found out that his daughter was Evelyn's rival. Now, right in front of him, at Elyse's side, lay *his* rival, triumphant, holding sway in his old bedroom.

Life was suddenly posing challenges Ernest had never expected. Frankly he wondered if it was possible, now that he was dead, to bear up under them. In the end, he was going to have to face a man, a disincarnate like himself, that he couldn't stand.

As best he could, he prepared for the encounter, tried to calm himself, and took a step forward. Without moving, his rival gave him a sarcastic glance. It was a look that bore the assurance of someone who had been expecting this moment for a long time.

In his dazed state Ernest didn't realize that someone else was aware of his presence as well. Elyse gave a terrible shout.

"Damn! Damn you!" she cried.

Her voice came out of the shadows of the room, dimly lit in the moonlight, and it sounded positively possessed.

"Get out of here, you demon," she yelled. "Get out! Murderer! Murderer! Help, Dede! Help! Take this man out of here! He's despicable. Despicable. Get out, Ernest! Get out! Killer! Killer!"

Hearing the commotion, Caio and Vera, terrified, came rushing in from Vera's bedroom. Vera turned on the lights and hurried over to her mother, who was still cursing Ernest and holding her head in her hands. The older woman looked petrified.

"Mother, what's wrong?" Vera asked, trying to soothe her. "We're here. You don't have to be afraid."

"Oh Vera, Vera!" the sick woman said, her chest heaving. "It's your father, the miserable sneak."

She held on to her daughter like a frightened child.

"Your father's here. Don't you understand?" There was no stopping Elyse's cries. "The scoundrel—he's in this room right now! I don't want to see him! Help me, for the love of God! Let's go back to São Paulo, tonight! Get me out of this house!"

She's deranged, Caio thought. She's gone completely out of her mind.

At the sight of his old love, Ernest wept as he never had. His tears fell in a tidal wave of suffering. How often he had dreamed of meeting Elyse again! How many times he had imagined himself as a bird far away from its nest and anxious to rest once again in the loving arms of its mate! And in the end, what had he found?—himself an unwanted guest, detested by his own family.

"Elyse," he begged. The troubled woman's psychic faculties had been upset by the switching on of the light, and she could no longer see her husband's form. His voice, though—moved, but still firm—she heard repeating steadily, "Elyse! Elyse, listen! I've always loved you."

In another moment, the two of them began talking to each other. It was an exchange of which her daughter and Caio could hear only one side, leaving the pair to stare down at the woman and then at each other, puzzled and afraid.

"Shut up, you monster," said Elyse, spitting out the words. "I don't want your love. I always detested what you call love."

Ernest asked, "Why did you change so much?"

"Today I can say whatever comes into my mind."

"But when we were together...."

"I was a slave, handcuffed to you—my lord and master."

"You always said you loved me."

"I've always despised you. That's the truth, if you really want to know."

"Oh! My God!"

"God? Look who's talking about God! A murderer."

"Why are you being cruel like this?"

"Dede told me you're nothing but a killer!"

The two incarnate listeners, following only Elyse's part of this conversation, had no idea what to make of it. By now, Caio had grown restless. Elyse's emotional frenzy had unsettled him, and he began looking around the house for a sedative to calm her nerves. The talk, however, went on without interruption.

"Listen, Elyse!" Ernest begged. "I know I did some awful things. But it was always because I needed you, because your affection drew me to you!"

"What a pack of lies!" She laughed, her tone hovering between madness and irony. "After you killed Dede, I started liking him even more. Whenever you came home, you made us very unhappy. Yes, we lived here together before your death, and we've been living together after it. Just look at this room! Dede is where he's always been!"

And with this she said things charity suggests be forever hidden.

Ernest cried. Lying just beyond him, his old enemy laughed, mocking him.

Meanwhile, Caio returned to the room, bringing with him a hypodermic needle. It contained an injection Vera used to help calm her mother whenever the sickness and delirium got out of hand.

In a few seconds Elyse had collapsed onto the bed, disheartened, her features distorted.

Ernest, about to leave, moved toward the door. In that instant, Desiderio Santos jumped out of the bed where he had been lying immobile. His mouth filled with a terrible shout, he blocked Ernest's way.

Chapter 20

PLOT DISCOVERED

"**Y**ou scoundrel! You coward," his rival yelled. He stood in front of Ernest, barring his path. "You're not getting away without us settling accounts! You thought all you had to do was put an end to me, huh? Let me tell you something—when you killed off my body, all you did was place me inside your own house. I live here now, and your wife is mine!"

Ernest, who'd struggled so much in life, had acquired a more cultivated attitude since his departure from earthly life.

"Desiderio! Can't you forgive me? I feel terrible for what I did."

"Forgive you?" said Desiderio. The more he spoke the more the mockery rose in his voice. "Don't count on it. I'm a long way from being finished with you, Ernest Fantini. You're going to pay, penny for penny, for what you did to me. Oh, I know you thugs. On Earth you try to excuse your murders. You talk about how sorry you are, and you think your phony tears are going to wash away the consequences. Well, nobody dies. You're just like any other criminal on Earth who thinks he can escape justice. But, believe me, you'll be punished by Divine Justice—and in your case, that justice is me. As far as you're concerned, I'm the spirit of revenge. And who can blame me?"

Desiderio was now worked up into a rage. In his tirade, he started crying tears of hate. "You idiots are all alike," he screamed. "You took my life, my home, my wife, my daughter. And now you expect me to reward you with forgiveness? You destroy a man, and you still want him to kiss your feet? You take advantage of the freedom of the grave that covers up your acts, and then ask defenseless victims for approval?"

Ernest was sobbing.

He clasped his hands together and knelt humbly before the man he had once vanquished. If only he had known before coming here what bitter trials would engulf his soul he would never have tried returning home. He would have put up with his longing for his wife and daughter, painful as it was, and used his energies elsewhere. But two years of study and meditation had taught him that, according to God's Law, each of us receives from life what he or she gives to it. No being, he knew, can escape his or her own conscience. The guilty must, at one point or another, face a day of atonement and readjustment.

Now, feeling the reality of this knowledge, he gave himself up to prayer. Jesus, he prayed, strengthen me so I can carry this cross, which I carved out through my own errors.

He remained kneeling at the house's entrance, looking up in his prayer toward the starry sky. Desiderio wasn't done with his accusations. "You coward," he spat. "Get up and face me like a man. We're on the same footing now. Twenty years ago you wanted to take my life away. Well, neither one of us is wearing the mask of the body now, are we? So, tell me, where's your arrogance, your lying smiles, your fast gun?"

"Desiderio—I didn't know!"

"Well, you ought to know one thing, you murdering wretch! I'm alive!"

"Yes," Ernest moaned, grimacing. "And I pray that God will forgive me for the evil thing I did to you."

"If God exists, He'll be on my side. You can't hide by calling on God."

"I know that. But I'm begging you, Desiderio—." The phrase stuck in his throat, choked by his pain and tears.

"Begging me for what?"

"Forgiveness—for the love you have for Elyse, and Elyse has for you! I never realized how involved my wife was with you. I'm a criminal, I know. But I became a criminal because I loved her so much. She was the wife God gave me!"

With this declaration, filled with contrition and humility, Ernest's cold-hearted enemy seemed to relent. It wasn't long, though, before the old hardness reasserted itself. "Why didn't you try getting rid of me some other

way? When you chose violence, all you did was drive
me deeper into your wife's arms. Even while you were
living in this house, after you thought I was dead, I was
sharing your table and your life. Sometimes you imagined you saw me, but you rationalized it away. You told
yourself that the image was a projection of your guilt.
You were wrong. What you were actually seeing, with
the eyes of your mind, was the real me, Desiderio Santos.
You were looking at me in the mirror of your own conscience—but looking at me all the same. You know, my
disembodied friends call me The Besetting Spirit. And
it's true. What else can I be? I am what I am—a humiliated man, the architect of my own revenge."

"Oh! Lord of Mercy, I'm the guilty one, the only
one responsible," said Ernest, overcome with self-loath-
ing..

Desiderio laughed aloud. "Oh, no, no," he said.
"You're not the only one! The murder was your idea
and you planned it. But the real killer was the man who
used you to get to me. I don't know why, but it's been
my lot to fall in with a bunch of assassins. You fired a
shot trying to end things between your wife and me.
You missed. Amancio, that low-life friend of yours, saw
that miss and took the opportunity to kill me and take
my wife. A couple of dark, devilish friends, you two
turned out to be—coming together like monsters to kill
me that morning!"

With this revelation, Ernest, despite the gnawing
sensation in his soul, recalled in all its detail the fatal
day he and his two companions had gone quail-hunt-

ing. Desiderio had been happy and confident; Amancio, worried about his two dogs, both trained retrievers; and he himself, lost in his plans for the crime. He especially remembered Amancio trying hard to control the dogs, which were excited at the prospect of the hunt. After a few short forays into the woods, where their shooting had come to nothing, Desiderio had shimmied up an old tree trunk, and holding himself erect between a couple of large branches, had aimed with his shotgun at a flock of birds flying overhead. Amancio was on one side of the tree, he on the other, with only a short distance separating them. Above them, Desiderio had his eyes on a bird flying away into the distance. He was listening to the bird's cries when Ernest, seeing his chance, raised his own gun, and shot him. Frightened, Ernest had then withdrawn into the bushes to await the immediate consequences of his act. He hadn't heard any shouts, though—only more shots, which he supposed came from Amancio's shotgun. Obviously the latter hadn't noticed his gunfire and was still hunting. A few minutes passed; then he had heard the scream from Amancio and the calls for help. He became alarmed, anxious, but managed to drag himself over to where Desiderio's dying body lay jerking convulsively. The sight of it had sickened him, but all he had been aware of at that moment was his terror at the deed he had just committed. It was because of his terror that he had latched on with relief to the explanation offered by Amancio who kept saying over and over again, "What a terrible accident! What a terrible accident!"

Accident! Hadn't that been the ideal explanation
to clear him? His hunting partner had given him a
strange look, as if accusing him. At the same time, without saying a word, Amancio had indicated his sympathy and understanding. Then Ernest remembered something else—the shot had entered beneath the jaws, exploding upward into the brain. That had seemed strange
at the time, but there had been no chance to examine
the body further.

The confusion that followed the murder had actually favored him. He found more balm for his conscience
when friends came by to see him in small groups. It was
an accident they all agreed. Of course, he had deliberately left out of his retelling any details that might have
made them suspect him or that would lead him to confess. But he took comfort wherever he could. With a
heavy heart, he remembered that, after Desiderio's funeral, he had cut all ties to Amancio, giving his grief as a
pretext. He had also decided to forget all about the
murdered man's wife and daughter, whose cries on that
unforgettable day had so troubled him, convinced as
he was that he was the only one responsible.

Numb with fright, Ernest realized that in a few seconds he had reconstructed all the details of the tragedy
in his mind.

Desiderio, as if watching him during every act of
this recollection, remained implacable. "That's right, you
miserable wretch, remember," he insisted. "Remember
how the two of you did it—just a couple of cynical killers. How could I have left my dead body without hat-

ing you? The suffering and revulsion drove me crazy. So when the spirit nurses[17] came to take me up in their arms and carry me away to I don't know where, I refused, sick to my stomach and sick at heart. The reality of an afterlife surprised me; I didn't necessarily want it. But since I had it, I decided I may as well use it for revenge.

"That was a long time ago, Ernest, and I'm not as angry as I was at first. But there's still hate burning in me, bitter hate. Enough to crush you! My trials poured over me like an avalanche. And here you are, playing the part of the good man, thinking that the only thing you have to do to clear your conscience is listen to my accusations!"

By this time, Desiderio had lost all control of himself. Cruelty, tears, pain, revulsion for Ernest, raged inside him and out. "Think how I must have felt," he went on. "I was disincarnated, but I came back to my young wife and little daughter, and found what? My murderer, Amancio, running over their lives. And here's something else. Do you suppose, Ernest, that I wanted your wife so much in the beginning? No. I didn't have any religious scruples, so I wasn't so sure about the morality of it—I had a wife and a daughter I adored—but I set my sights on Elyse anyway. She was a devoted and distinguished lady and, like a fool, I was attracted by all her

---

[17] *Translator's Note: Spirit nurses: those who provide initial assistance, treatment, and guidance in the initial stages of one's adaptation to the afterlife.*

attentions. Still, all you would have had to do was act like a real friend and be honest with me about it; I would have backed off. But your jealousy blinded you, and you tried to kill me like a wild animal. Your plan changed me into a beast free of its jail of skin and bones. After my death, Amancio very quickly married Brigitte, the woman I left widowed and inexperienced. I couldn't stand the sight of him.

"Soon enough I felt myself being pushed out of my own house, my refuge. Hating him, I felt in my own house a rage that forced me to leave it. I was like a dog without an owner that's been beaten and driven off. I missed my wife, but she had erased me from her memory. I missed my daughter, but she had to kiss my executioner like a second father. I roamed around the streets with the mobs from the darkness. Finally I found my way to your wife and became her constant companion. Her love kept calling and calling me, and little by little, from a spiritual point of view, I adjusted myself to her like a foot to a shoe. And I fell deeply in love with her, because she was the only being in the world who kept me in her heart and memory."

Desiderio paused, needing rest after this outburst. Ernest tried to beg for mercy, but the words died in his throat. His whole soul trembled. He was like a criminal at his own trial, but unable to mount a defense.

After a while Desiderio regained his strength. "And what was all this for?" He continued, relentless as ever, "Guilt stunted your mind. From the time I lost my body, you were always on the lookout for an escape. It was impossible. You threw yourself into business and money-making, into deals and contracts, and you were constantly traveling. So you had no time to give your wife and daughter the help and tenderness they needed. All of that turned my affection for Elyse into something more than earthly liking. The Besetting Spirit? Oh, yes, I am that. But I'm the unconditional servant of the woman who bears your name, and who put up so long with that cold heart of yours. I learned patience and how to be silent, waiting with your wife. And your daughter? Did you even know about your daughter's illnesses when she was a child? Did you know how hard her early teenage years were for her, and how many temptations she faced? Did you know about the boys who took advantage of her? Did you, at any time, dry her tears after those same boys publicly laughed at her innocence and tenderness? Ernest, Ernest—you never brought yourself to that level of suffering at home. But I know the cross your wife carried as she grew older, and the one your daughter carried as she grew up, both of them crying. Why did you come back to this house? To reap the love you didn't sow? To settle accounts?"

Broken in the face of these charges, Ernest managed to stammer out, "Desiderio, I understand now. Please forgive me!"

But at the sight of Ernest's pain his rival grew more and more excited , and returned to the attack. "I suffered for your daughter and for mine, the little girl I lost at my death. Brigitte had all the faith in the world in that scoundrel Amancio. He became her whole world.

To please him she agreed to give up our little daughter—had her put in a boarding school. She apparently got a good education. But she also suffered as much from losing her parents as if she had been abandoned at birth. What I've been through, Ernest, what I've been through! You can't imagine it. But my suffering didn't stop there. My poor little daughter grew up sad and without moral support. She lacked the guidance of her father, the one you and Amancio robbed her of, and she died two years ago exactly. She was pushed by her stepfather, who only wanted to get rid of his responsibility for her, and much too early she married a crazy man who destroyed all her dreams. Oh, I worked hard to stop her marriage to that coward. I was always running back and forth between your family and mine, full of despair and trying to avoid the tragedy that finally occurred.

"As I say, she died. I went to see her, along with some disincarnate friends who were suffering and forsaken as I was. I knelt down by her motionless body—her lips still carried her last smile—and I swore to take revenge on the three hypocrites standing by her: the murderer Amancio, the ingrate Brigitte, the detestable son-in-law, whose presence makes me sick. I cried and asked God for the grace of seeing my daughter free of her physical suffering, for the happiness of hearing her voice. But the spirit nurses told me she had been taken to a resting place. I would be allowed to see her again only when I had cured the sores of revolt I carried inside me—as if I could ever stop the pain of the fire that

burns here! My poor daughter—she married a criminal. It was as if she had to share in my destiny as a wandering spirit. Oh, don't think I wouldn't love to put out
these flames, Ernest—but it's impossible!"

Ernest, speechless, could only sigh and shake his
head.

Desiderio, his former friend, went on, as if trying
to pour out all the bitterness of his soul on him. "But
there's one more thing you need to know," he said. "I
saw my daughter grow sick and disheartened because
of her unhappy home life, and then her husband started
cheating on her. He came to know Vera Celine, your
daughter, and won her love. Then he dominated her,
enslaved her. " He pointed inside the house. "Understand this, Ernest: the bastard is here right now. His
name is Caio Serpa. That's right, Ernest—Ah...Evelyn,
Evelyn... my daughter!... My child!"

Ernest, hearing Desiderio speak the names of
Evelyn and Caio made all the connections. He felt his
brain explode with anguish. He jumped up, and even
as he asked for Jesus's blessings and Rivas's protection,
ran to a clump of nearby bushes, unable to stop his cries.
Not caring what he did, he threw himself down on the
sandy ground of the island, and there, like a beaten dog,
wept in pain.

Chapter 21

RETURN TO THE PAST

The memory of Rivas's warnings and Evelyn's presence nearby finally allowed Ernest to establish some semblance of self-control. He had gone through a tear-filled crisis, and at the end of it he was surprised to find Evelyn occupying a new position in his inner world. He found himself changed. The innermost recesses of his mind had been reconfigured. Desiderio's criticism, frank and free, had shaken him, and for the first time the extent of his own feebleness was apparent to him. True, it had shaken his pride. But it had also left the very core of his heart clear, so he saw that it might be possible now to seek a new life.

Still a little stunned, he got up off the ground and dragged himself to the place where Evelyn was waiting for him.

Evelyn was having a friendly conversation with some disembodied patients. They were visiting the area under nurses' care, and taking advantage of certain nutritive emanations from the sea.

Seeing Ernest so unsteady on his feet, she ran to meet him.

"Ernest, what has happened? You look so shaken." Her voice was tinged with anxiety. Gently, she helped him sit down on the sand.

He didn't refuse her support, and as soon as she sat next to him, he put his head in his hands. It was the gesture of someone whose thoughts were on fire, and who was having trouble accepting them. "Evelyn, Evelyn!" he stammered, his tears returning. "I know it now—we are among the dead that no one on Earth prayed for. My God! The hearts I loved most are closed to me forever. They're as sealed off to me as the grave that holds my body. I'm leaving my house a condemned man, Evelyn. My God, my God!"

She tried to console him, remembering her own experience a few hours earlier. But Ernest was desolate. Out of his own deep pain, he resisted her assurances. "No, no," he insisted. "You were the victim of an ungrateful man. I received the blame I deserve. You got the insult, I got the punishment."

Ernest wanted very much to tell her what had happened, to confide what he knew; but his strength was waning, and the waves of tears kept coming. To the relief of both, transportation arrived shortly at the Mar Casado Beach to take them back to São Paulo. With the sight of it, their confusion and misery lessened a bit. Rivas had heard the prayers of his tortured student and sent urgent orders that both his wards be attended to immediately.

Evelyn helped Ernest into the craft, which was soon on its way. She tried talking to him, but he replied only in monosyllables, preferring to keep quiet, though his look, sad and fixed, gave evidence of the volcano of contradictory feelings exploding inside him.

Following Rivas's instructions, the travelers were taken to a resting place in a Christian Spiritist Center in São Paulo. There, Ernest's trauma was given the proper healing treatment—magnetic healing in a circle of prayer—which helped calm him down. With Evelyn's help, he started to recuperate. As soon as his energies were in harmony again, he asked her, with a tone of great sadness in his voice, "Evelyn, was Desiderio Santos your father's name, and is Amancio Terra your stepfather?"

"That's right. My full name is Evelyn dos Santos Serpa."

Ernest didn't hold back then. He knew he owed her a complete confession. He started with his memories of his marriage to Elyse. He could only sketch in some of these scenes but, to her growing surprise, they came out one by one: his closeness to Desiderio since childhood; his superficial knowledge of Brigitte, whom he met only a few times; his friendship with Amancio, who had always wanted to remain single. He spoke of Desiderio's frequent visits to his house, which were never returned; of the attraction his guest excited in Elyse, the wife he loved deeply; of his jealousy as he watched the two becoming closer. He told her about the plan to eliminate Desiderio, whom he started to detest, and the silent contempt that poisoned all his feelings. He described the sinister hunt, the shot he intentionally fired, and the other shots he heard; Dede's death and the guilt that ruined his entire life. Finally, he took her, step-by-step, through the episode of his return home, from the instant Elyse, in a violent crisis, began insulting him up to Desiderio's last statement, which had all but destroyed him.

In vain, Evelyn searched her brain for words to describe her astonishment. Not that Ernest's story drove her away from him; she offered him, as always, a respectful and tender love. But she found it so strange—this complex drama in which they were, unknowingly, the protagonists. The turns of the plot built around these two families surprised and fascinated her. Her pity at all the intimate conflicts involved in the tragedy overwhelmed her. In the end she concluded she was the one least affected by it all.

She stared at Ernest and began crying softly.

As he looked at her, suffering so silently and with such dignity through the pain caused to her soul, he asked anxiously: "Do you blame me, too?"

"Oh no, Ernest," she answered. "Our friendship is stronger than ever. I'm the one, your sister, who's asking you to forgive my father, who took over your house. He stole from you, he wronged you."

"No, he didn't steal anything," Ernest said, touched by her generosity. "He protected the wife and daughter I neglected. And talking about excuses; please, will you make allowances for my daughter, who took your husband."

"No, no! I understand that Vera came into my path as a benefactor ." It was now Evelyn's turn to justify the girl. "She gave Caio the security I couldn't."

"Evelyn," he said, feeling more relieved, "today I've seen that it's only in the life after death that we manage to undo the horrible mistakes we made on Earth."

She agreed and they carried on this soul-baring *tête-à-tête* until Ernest finally became drowsy and asked her to excuse him while he took a nap.

Morning came. At the appointed hour their transportation arrived to pick them up for the return journey.

Evelyn wanted very much to see her father, but Ernest thought it would be prudent for her not to try it without more preparation. Both of them felt better, almost restored—so much so that during the trip they kept debating, as did their fellow passengers, the fundamental questions of life: love, reincarnation, home, the need for suffering.

Back home in the spiritual colony, they kept dreaming about the future, talking and planning together. Wouldn't it be better for Tulio to be reborn with Caio and Vera, whose marriage they would approve? Evelyn, always generous, also remembered her father and his suffering. If she could and if circumstances allowed, she would love to work with him, to get him to give up his revenge and accept a reincarnation, so that he could forget.

She and Ernest marveled now at how they wanted more and more time for their loved ones on Earth. They would pray for them. They would ask God to extend their time in the physical world, in the interest of the family group, and their own interest. Evelyn could imagine seeing Tulio in Caio's home and the two of them becoming reconciled. Ernest agreed, saying that the possibility of bringing Amancio and Desiderio together had to be analyzed, so they could change their hatred into empathy, their antagonism into union.

In this way, the pair dreamed on.

Ten days went by after their return from São Paulo before the two felt completely restored. They asked then for a meeting with Rivas in order to let him in on their new ideas and to comment on what had happened.

Rivas received them with his usual politeness, and listened to their plans intently. To their surprise, he answered briefly rather than give the more extensive answers they had hoped for. "When Ernest's prayers reached us," he said, "we not only gave you the help you needed but we also asked for notes on all the family events you were part of. Our documents revealed everything you have come to know. As for moral duties, I think you understood them well enough from our meetings. You have the necessary guidance. You have reached the point now, I'm sure you can appreciate, where we intend to go full speed ahead with the spiritual work—work you have requested many times, as a matter of fact."

"Is it fair to continue acting on loved ones' behalf?"

asked Ernest. He wanted, sincerely, to be correct in the matter.

"My friend, it's our duty," replied Rivas. "Those who know need to help those who don't—and not simply help, but help with love."

"Would it be all right to visualize reincarnations for Tulio and my father in the near future?" Evelyn asked, a little timidly.

"Why not, my child? But for that we have to arrange concrete data and match it with exact planning. Before Divine Providence we're all one family, all interconnected, and it's our duty to help each other. Evolution is our slow walk back to God. The ones who love the most lead and mark the way for their brothers and sisters."

"We would appreciate some guidance, some counsel, in getting started," said Ernest, who didn't want Rivas to think of him as someone who simply took things into his own hands.

"We need some up-to-date information," said Rivas, "so today I'm sending an impartial observer to São Paulo to look over the general situation of the individuals involved in this case. Meanwhile, the two of you might want to visit the southern part of the state tomorrow. You need to meet the family members you weren't able to see. When you return tomorrow evening, we'll study the matter more carefully. By then we'll have accurate news that should clarify the situation for us."

And with these words, he adjourned the meeting.

The next day, using the regular transportation from

the spiritual city to the physical world, the two friends arrived in the suburbs of the city where Amancio had built his home.

Followed by Ernest, Evelyn made her way through the gateway of her old home. In many ways, it was like a sweet return to her childhood. It seemed she might have been coming back to this sunny house as she used to do on a school holiday, eager for affection. She could see, farther away, the abundant groves, and nearer, the gate covered with wild bindweed. A few steps away was an enormous patio spread outward in the direction of a large yard that was used in the processing of coffee beans.

Holding Ernest's arm, she walked to the entryway, held spellbound by her memories. She crossed the threshold with the awe of someone going into a place sacred to her heart. It was the same peaceful environment. The living room with its old furniture stirred gentle memories: the heirloom her mother was so proud to have inherited from her grandparents; the rugs made from the skins of wild cats shot by Amancio while hunting in Mato Grosso[18]; the five-lamp chandeliers hanging from the ceiling; the piano at which she had so often listened in ecstasy to her mother's renditions of Chopin.

One surprise did await her and it filled her with happiness. On top of the piano, next to some forgotten

---

[18] *Translator's Note: State in the central region of Brazil.*

musical compositions, sat a picture of her as a teenager, and next to it, a discolored rose symbolizing maternal love.

Evelyn ran to the veranda at the side of the house where Amancio and her mother used to relax after meals. There she found them in quiet conversation, each sitting on a favorite couch. At the sight, she had no words for her emotions. Overcome, she knelt down before her mother in whose face she saw more wrinkles, framed by many more streaks of gray hair. She put her head on the woman's lap, and cried convulsively, as she once did at the frustrations and inexplicable thoughts of her youth.

Brigitte was not directly aware of her presence. She did, however, fix her dreaming gaze on some nearby trees, and suddenly felt an inexpressible longing for her daughter. Tears welled up in her eyes. "I wish, I so wish, I could see my darling Evelyn!" she said.

The very person about whom she was thinking answered, "Mother! Mommy, I'm here!"

After one or two minutes of silence, Amancio gazed over at his wife and asked, "Why did you stop talking, dear? What are you thinking about?"

His voice was full of tenderness. He obviously hadn't lost any of his devotion to his wife after their marriage. The softness of his tone surprised Ernest.

"I don't know how to explain it, Amancio," Brigitte said, "but I've been longing so much for our daughter. Two years of absence——." Then, a little more focused, she added, "Why did she have to leave us so early in life?"

"Oh, you old mother hen," her husband objected affectionately. "The past won't come back. We can't do anything about it except try to forget."

"I believe there's another life where people who loved one another deeply in this world will meet again."

"That's what the philosophers say," answered Amancio, trying to be helpful. "However, the practical men say, with good reason, that the only thing we know about the dead is their death certificates."

At this moment, Ernest touched the man on the head, as if to confirm an unspoken suspicion. Sure enough, locked deep in the recesses of his mind, he found the scene of Desiderio's murder as he himself remembered it. Something told him, though, that it would be wrong to stir up anything negative in his old friend's spirit. It would be useless, especially when everything around him indicated that Amancio had become a man on whom a number of families in the area depended for work. Ernest saw he wasn't just devoted and tender to a woman who had once been his victim but, from the number of satisfied-looking workers gathered around his house, he was a well-thought-of employer and manager. Besides, who was he to throw the first stone? The only reason he hadn't killed Desiderio himself was his poor aim. Before God and his own conscience, wasn't he as guilty as his old friend, who had managed to hit his target?

These thoughts were burning in his mind when he heard Evelyn, in tears, speaking directly to her mother's heart: "Oh! Mommy, now I know Father is carrying so much hate in a world of shadows. What can we do to help him?"

Until then, Brigitte hadn't thought of her first husband; in fact, she had registered nothing outright except a vague, painful yearning to go back to the past, but without recalling Desiderio. However, her daughter insisted: "Help, Mommy. Help Father return to the physical life! Who knows? Father Amancio and you live alone in this house. Think of it—a boy, a child of the heart!"

At this point in Evelyn's plea, her mother was seized by the idea of her second husband and herself getting old, without descendants. It occurred to her that a child, adopted by them, would be a support for the future. Prompted by Evelyn, she started to concentrate on a boy; someone to fill their lives with new hope, to continue the work they had started on that small piece of land.

Evelyn kept reinforcing this thought, sending to her mother's soul her own messages of agreement until, enthusiastic as her daughter, Brigitte decided to sound out her husband on the matter.

"Amancio, I think so much about our old age, and how lonely we'll be. But there are lots of possibilities to remedy that. For instance, maybe we can adopt a boy. He'll be like the son we never had."

"At our age! What an idea!"

"We're not that old—."

"Oh! Come on, Brigitte, you can't be serious—the

idea is ridiculous! Wouldn't it be bizarre to come to the end of our lives and find ourselves making bottles for a baby?"

"But it could be just the opposite. What if God gives us a long, long time here on Earth? What if we had a brave boy here to leave the farm to—someone to carry on the business we've built."

"Well, I'm not so optimistic," Amancio told her.

At the same time, there was tenderness and generosity in his voice. "Still," he said. "I've always liked your whims, and I'm not all that opposed to what you want. But let's get one thing straight—he's got to be a little boy, brought up here from birth, without any interfering parents—and he should cry as little as possible. That's all, as long as you don't complain about the extra work."

"Oh Amancio, how happy you've made me!"

Brigitte was jubilant, transformed with happiness, and her husband too felt a mysterious elation rise up from his inner being.

Evelyn had stood up, gone over to him, kissed his gray hair, and at the same time laid her right hand on his chest, as if caressing his heart.

Chapter 22

THE BASIS FOR A NEW FUTURE

E rnest and Evelyn conferred with Rivas the following day. They gave him a succinct account of the visit, to which he listened carefully. Then, trying to use the time effectively, he asked for a set of files stored in a nearby cabinet, and started the most important task of the interview, analyzing Tulio Mancini's situation. In his view, the young man had shown very little progress. This didn't, however, cancel out Evelyn's duty of seeing him through his next rebirth. Her support of him, said Rivas, shouldn't waver.

The instructor then set up the basis for the future work, sketching out a program of immediate and more clearly defined action for them both. It required that their efforts be both precise and effective. Evelyn would continue working alone with Tulio, and keep encouraging his mental renewal as much as possible. On a daily basis Ernest would go to the physical plane where, as best he could, he would assist in helping Desiderio and Elyse, who needed urgent and constant attendance. Rivas also arranged with various service directors in the Higher Spheres for authority to resolve whatever problems might arise with any of the rebirths considered necessary to the harmony of the family group.

Evelyn, having received her instructions, said sadly, "Instructor Rivas, I won't be allowed to visit my father and take him to my heart? You do understand how I long for him?"

"Yes, I know, but in Desiderio's present condition, he can't handle spontaneous feelings of that kind. If we're going to help him with confidence, we first have to examine all our previous attitudes, the smallest ones included."

"Even mine?"

"Yes, your reactions as a daughter also enter into the equation. Your father has a rebellious nature, but a noble heart. He has many fine qualities that will blossom when the time comes. Think, my child; we shouldn't risk botching our opportunities with Desiderio by acting too soon. Be patient."

"How can I?"

"Your father has to meet you again in a moment of higher understanding. Ernest will help him on a daily basis with his edifying words. His is a task similar to the domestic situation you're working for in trying to help Tulio—to waken him to the joys of a blissful spiritual life. While Ernest carries out this task, he and Desiderio will learn to regain mutual respect and affection." With a friendly smile, Rivas added, "Isn't that what's happening with Tulio and you?"

Evelyn understood and agreed.

"This won't stop you from intervening in events when circumstances call for it. You can, and ought to, see your father again. But your influence as his daughter has to be used for his own benefit."

Evelyn said no more, and Ernest asked the next question. "Instructor, I hope this isn't inappropriate, but I wonder if your messenger has reported on the situation of our friends in Guarujá?"

"Yes, but they weren't there. They're in São Paulo."

"At the house in Vila Mariana?"

"Caio and Vera, yes."

"How about Elyse?"

"Placed in a sanitarium for the mentally ill six days ago."

"My God, how things change!"

"Caio urged Vera to take responsibility for her, so she did; and Elyse, being sick, couldn't put up much of a fight. We have received news, though, that her physical prognosis is very serious. I have to tell you that she's in a very serious condition. Her obsessive mental state and her weak circulatory system suggest a progressive cerebral thrombosis. Chances are that she'll have a stroke and expire very shortly. All because of a terrible disappointment."

Startled, Ernest asked, "What disappointment?"

"Caio has been pressing Vera for a few weeks now to take over the management of her mother's affairs," the instructor answered calmly. "He's a lawyer and has a good many contacts. He used his influence, and as soon as he convinced his future mother-in-law to go into the hospital—he assured her she wouldn't be there for more than two or three days—he drew up the necessary documents and got them notarized. He told their friends that he was doing all this for the sake of Vera, his wife-to-be. Well, you can imagine what a painful shock it was to Elyse when she realized at the hospital that she no longer had control of her finances. She might be under the influence of a disturbing spirit, but she's perfectly lucid. She's going through a tortured mediumship, with psychic phenomena none of the people around her comprehend. We understand this, but to Caio and Vera, she's just a case of advanced senility."

"Caio, then . . . now . . ." the phrase died on Ernest's tongue.

"Has power of attorney," said Rivas, finishing the thought, "over both her and Vera—legal power to manage all their property." Evelyn and Ernest looked at each other, astonished. "In view of these facts," Rivas continued, "and because our new understanding demands it, I have to tell you, Ernest, that Caio sold off your land in Santos the day before yesterday. He now finds himself with a lot of extra money, although he pretends it's a commission for the sale. I'm not telling you this as a judge of his behavior, but because we need to plan for the future, and we have to know how to deal with undesirable details like this."

"What a thief!" Ernest's accusation showed how little reconciled he was to this particular detail. "My God! So we're faced with Caio the criminal again."

Rivas gave him a fatherly look and demurred: "Let's avoid any thoughts of cruelty or violence," he said. "We need to involve both Caio and Vera with our empathetic thoughts."

"Why?" Ernest was despondent.

"Because, by providence, both of you are now the particular friends of this family group. If you work confidently to give Caio the emotional support he very much needs, he'll marry Vera and become Tulio's father in the future. If he does, he will, without a doubt, pay off his debts. Having taken Tulio's physical life, he'll be forced to restore that life, according to the law of cause and effect. Besides, he'll bring peace to Evelyn by taking responsibility in the physical world for reeducating an emotionally disturbed spirit who's put her through so much."

"I understand all that, but...." Ernest searched for another argument.

"I know what you're thinking, Ernest," Rivas said, interrupting. "You're still attached to the blood family the Lord loaned you on Earth, and you realize that Caio has started taking control of your considerable fortune. But don't delude yourself. In the same way he sold your land in Santos, he'll dispose of your rental apartments in São Paulo, your house in Guarujá, your life insurance money, your jewels, your bank accounts, and even the house in Vila Mariana. You have to accept the reality of it, my friend. After you died, all your property on Earth passed into the control of other people. Life asks for what it loaned us, and in return it gives us what we made of it, whatever and wherever that may be. All the changes we spoke of will come about as soon as Caio marries your daughter. But let's not call him a thief and criminal. He's a child of God, just as we are, borrowing from the future. Today he's borrowing from Elyse and Vera the resources you left them—the fruit of your enormously productive life. He thinks he's very intelligent and has pulled off a brilliant coup. But the person he's deceiving, this poor friend, is himself."

"How can that be?"

"He thinks he's controlling vast assets," said Rivas, continuing to clarify the situation. "In fact, before the Divine Laws, Caio is only assuming large debts. By keeping Elyse's and Vera's inheritance, he has the means of experiencing, instinctively, the hunger for more wealth. He'll fall in love with money, and pretty soon, he'll be trapped. Instead of finding joy in the simple life, he'll move a long way away from true happiness. For a long time he'll be a slave to the need to earn and earn, accumulate and accumulate. And in the end, all this will revert to the benefit of —who do you think?"

"I have no idea," said Ernest.

"Of your family, Ernest," returned the instructor, "and especially Elyse, though he's currently driving her to a premature death with all his foolish comments, eager as he is to control her finances without suffering any consequences."

"Oh? Could you please explain that?" Ernest felt suddenly anxious to know how his family could benefit.

Rivas, who had been examining some papers as he spoke, pulled out a small map, and pointing to graphs here and there, he said, "Elyse's last breath is expected in a few days. According to our plans, her rebirth—after a harmonizing period here—should occur in five or six years. We already have permission from our Elders, and if you work hard to help both of them, and do it with a lot of love, she'll be Caio's and Vera's daughter. She'll be reborn after Tulio, who'll be their first born. In about thirty years, more or less—as you can see here— Caio will return to the spiritual life. And he'll leave to the mother-in-law he's plundering (she'll be his daughter by then), and to Vera Celine, his widow, everything he's taking today. Not only that, but the value of it will be enormously increased. He'll also have worked hard to leave his heir, Tulio in his new existence, considerable material wealth."

These evidences of the safety of God's laws left Evelyn and Ernest astonished.

Now, Rivas was bringing the conference to an end. "So let's not characterize Caio as a thief or criminal," he warned. "Actually, he's our ally, our friend. What we have to do, immediately, is pray to God to give him good physical health and a sense of spiritual well-being, so he can live relatively peacefully in his earthly cocoon for many years to come." He then added, smiling, "A time will come when both of you will, as much as you can, prepare yourselves to protect his personal assets and increase his profits as a way of protecting the future of your loved ones. Let's ask God to make him a rich and kind man, hard working, with all sorts of accomplishments to his credit. We need him, and he needs us."

Seeing the conversation almost over, Evelyn quickly asked, "Instructor, how about my father? I've been dreaming of a rebirth for him."

"He's part of our plan, too," the instructor replied. "We know, Evelyn, what a loving daughter you are, and realized you would try to help him. We were told that yesterday you inserted a seed-idea in your mother's heart, asking her to receive him as an adopted son. With Divine Help, that will come about. It was a very worthy appeal, and it'll help Amancio Terra get the help he deserves. It's true he was once blinded by passion and killed your father's body. He also took his house and money. The man is an atheist and evidently a criminal. But, odd as it might seem, he's also very humane and charitable. He stole your father's property, true. But he's a good businessman. He expanded that property, and provided economic support for more than two hundred people—his laborers and tenant farmers, and their descendants. He's been protecting them all like a good, caring father for over twenty years. He has never abandoned the sick ones, never fired the slow ones, never let any child go hungry. Yes, he murdered your father, and he'll answer for it in the court of life. But he is dedicated to your mother, and like a good, honest husband he tries to satisfy her every wish. He spreads so much comfort and joy, and so many prayers for him come from Earth to the Infinite Mercy of God, that he has earned a great deal of consideration from our Elders. We were advised yesterday, by the way, that your request will be answered when the time is right. As far as your father is concerned, he'll return with God's blessings, as you asked, to live with the man he still hates. But he'll come to see Amancio's first-rate qualities and even to love him as a father. Amancio will sacrifice for him, give him love and support, and provide an excellent example."

Rivas was silent for a few moments. Then, as if answering the doubts of his listeners, he said in an emphatic tone, "Amancio only has ten more years in the physical body, according to the information we have. But for a man with a record of service like his, it won't be hard to convince the Superior Powers to stay that, and give him an extra fifteen or twenty years in his present life. In view of all that, we hope he can actually accept from the Lord the happiness of having Desiderio as a son. Desiderio will be reborn into the home of a poor couple, but Amancio will give him a new life and eventually restore everything he once took from him. You can be sure, Evelyn, that the very man who killed your father will guide him in a new direction. Amancio has learned the value of hard work and he has changed into a worker of good. Desiderio will have everything he needs to be a reasonable and happy man."

Rivas now revealed something else. "Our plan calls for an important event. Very soon now, we'll be called on to bring Caio's and Amancio's homes close to each other since Desiderio and Elyse, in their reincarnated lives, will marry young—and have a very happy marriage. So let's do our best to ensure that Desiderio returns to the physical life in the shortest time possible."

Evelyn, thinking about God's perfect justice, was crying with happiness. Ernest, amazed and thrilled at once, admired the logic of the plan Rivas had laid out for them.

Drying her tears, Evelyn managed a new question, "How about my mother?"

"Brigitte will share Amancio's destiny," the instructor answered. "Desiderio, your biological father, married her, but he didn't love her. In fact, according to our records and reports, even while you were in the cradle he was already chasing other women."

"All these projects," said Ernest in wonder. "You know, turning a slab of marble into a work of art requires a huge amount of work. Who is going to be responsible for carrying out all these plans?"

Rivas gave him a kindhearted look and said to both of them, "Have you ever heard of spirit guides?"

Ernest and Evelyn, surprised by the question, looked at him blankly.

"Well," Rivas explained, "both of you will be in charge of this venture, together with all the related tasks that go along with it. You'll make sure Caio and Vera get married; that Elyse gets well as soon as possible after passing on; that Desiderio is reborn in favorable conditions. You'll help Elyse return to Earth, and protect her during her infancy and childhood—in addition to assisting with Desiderio's future biological mother and making sure she has the resources she needs to assure a safe birth. You'll also ease Desiderio's reincarnation so that he'll be ready to accept his position as an adopted son. And let's not forget about Tulio, who needs special attention. Then there's his future guidance, and later the marriage between Elyse and Desiderio—that is, after the measures we take to ensure the meeting between the Terra and Serpa families." He finished with a comical shrug and a little smile. "That's work for more than thirty years, friends. So you might as well start thinking of yourselves as citizens of the city. You have a job here for the next thirty years at least!"

Deeply affected, Ernest gazed over at Evelyn, and thought sadly about how they both had been erased from the minds of the people they loved most—how they had practically been forgotten, or rejected, or sent away, or replaced. On the same wave-length with these ideas and feelings, Evelyn gazed back. She felt frankly that Caio's attitudes had released her from any further intimate relationship with him. Now, she and Ernest would be working together exclusively in an enterprise that would require close collaboration. For his part, Ernest's suffering during the last few days seemed to have spiritualized him, as if the fire of the trials he had endured had renewed his form and revitalized his features. Both felt their consciences at peace.

The two looked at each other and understood. Their loved ones on Earth, except for Brigitte, who still longed for her daughter, had abandoned them. Nonetheless, they needed to act and to build—for their own benefit. Like allies, coming together again on the field of life in an undertaking both held dear, they promised each other, wordlessly, to link hearts, to transfer to each other the sacred treasures of love they had brought with them. More than ever, they were convinced, they needed each other's support for the long journey ahead. A journey that was also an answer to their genuine desire for redemption.

Chapter 23

ERNEST IN SERVICE

Ernest's and Evelyn's spiritual work went forward confidently. On the one hand, they tried to encourage improvements in Tulio and on the other to relocate Desiderio, who refused to leave Elyse (now under treatment and relegated to her own thoughts at a sanitarium).

Ernest's work was becoming increasingly difficult. His rival never missed a chance to accuse and mock him, and Elyse's physical condition was worsening every day. His efforts to get closer to her had come to nothing. The situation worried him. He called on Rivas and explained the problem.

How had a suffering spirit, hardened by ideas of revenge, acquired such powers of discernment that he could point out the smallest defects in Ernest's character?

"Ah, my friend!" answered the instructor. "When resentment and hatred govern people, their arrows al-

ways seem to hit our open wounds—especially if we
have set ourselves up as idols with feet of clay."

"Why is that?"

"We often take on roles in the world that we don't
fill well. We wear labels—Husband, Parent, Child, Ad-
ministrator. But we don't always bother with the obligations the roles entail. Do you understand? I was a la-
bel-wearing husband on Earth myself. I married, I took
on family responsibilities. But I thought my responsibilities ended with playing the head-of-household role,
and paying the bills at the end of the month. I never
shared my wife's concern over our children's upbring-
ing. As far as I can remember, I never once sat down
with them and listened to their problems and dreams,
even though I demanded a high standard of conduct
from them—one that wouldn't reflect badly on me."

Ernest noted the gentle reproach in these words,
and found himself once again prodded by his conscience. He had to admit that, yes, he hadn't been the
husband and father he should have been. Only here,
in this spiritual colony and after the death of his physical body, had he come to understand, during his hard-
est battles of self-correction, that money can't do the
heart's job.

He felt dejected, depressed, and didn't pursue the
subject of the meeting any further. As he left, Rivas lingered awhile at the door, offering what comfort he could.

"Don't despair," he said. "Let's listen to what our
opponents throw at us, and try to use their criticisms—
to the extent that they're true and helpful—with hu-

mility. That is the key, Ernest, humility. It works in solving our biggest, most puzzling problems, and it's unfailing. Let's be authentic Christians by loving, serving, and forgiving."

Thereafter, with this lesson in mind, Ernest dedicated himself more and more to real fellowship, whether it was by putting up with his sick wife's diatribes, or resigning himself to Desiderio's taunts. He was always ready for a verbal beating.

After twenty-six days of projecting the correct thought waves into Caio's particular field of action, he found, to his surprise, that Caio was coming for the first time to visit his future mother-in-law.

The lawyer, neatly dressed, stood in front of the patient. They met in a private room—courtesy of the sanitarium's administration—where, Caio said, he wanted to get an accurate picture of the woman, so as to have some positive feedback to give his fiancée. With the two of them stood the disincarnate spirits, Desiderio and Ernest, both anxious to see the results of the interview.

Once Caio and Elyse were alone together Elyse told him, as calmly as she could, that she wanted more than anything to see her daughter. Vera would see for herself that she wasn't crazy and take her home. The humility with which she made this request, as a woman bowed down by circumstance, touched both Ernest and Desiderio.

Caio, however, remained firm. "Absolutely not," he said. "Your case won't allow it. You can't be released right now."

"Why not?"

"Your behavior doesn't justify us taking you out."

"Behavior? What behavior?"

"You keep crying for no reason. You talk to your-self, to shadows."

"You simply don't understand me. What I see, I see."

"Vera calls every day and the nurses tell her your condition is the same."

"Despite all that, Caio," said Elyse, the nervousness showing in her voice, "I insist that you, as a gentleman, bring Vera to see me."

"Why? So you can traumatize her with your fanta-sies? Don't you think your daughter has suffered enough with all your crying and keeping her up all night?"

"Oh, Caio!"

"You know very well that I'm almost your son-in-law. I have the right to interfere."

"I don't know if anyone has the right to come be-tween a mother and her child," she answered. In her words was a well of sadness. "I'm not arguing with your management of household affairs, to the point where I can't even write a simple check . . ."

"Oh, stop complaining," Caio interrupted sharply. "I accepted the role of your lawyer to please your daughter. I have enough work to do without being your employee."

"I'm not complaining, and I do think you're looking out for my daughter's interest. But in my case..."

"What do you mean?"

"In my case, neither of you will have to worry long. Just a few feet of ground."

"Quit talking like that. What's so important? We all die. And if you're going on like this to play on my sympathy, forget it."

"My God, I just want to see my daughter!"

"Until you start acting normally and having a more positive attitude, the answer is no."

"But why? Haven't I always welcomed you in my house as a son?"

"That's a lie. You hate me. The only reason you didn't show me the door was because Vera wouldn't let you. Because I'm the man she chose to share her future." Then, to Elyse's pain and astonishment, he added, "And you'd better realize that we're both sick of this. You've already lived your life and now you're trying to ruin ours. Well, no aging mother-in-law is going to spoil our plans."

Hot anger stirred in Elyse. "You're despicable," she shouted.

Desiderio, the discarnate spirit who usually controlled her mind, now took advantage of this outburst of indignation to regain command of it, this time spectacularly.

A crisis ensued.

Elyse, possessed, attacked her visitor. She tried to choke him. She cursed him in words that in her mouth sounded strange and awful indeed.

Caio, astonished, backed away from her. A nurse, hearing the commotion, came into the room. Quickly she sized up the state of things, and grabbed firm hold of Elyse from behind. On the other side, Ernest similarly gained control over the wildly struggling Desiderio.

In a matter of moments, order had been reestablished.

With two aides helping her, the nurse led Elyse back to her room, then came back to explain. "Don't worry, sir. It's just another one of her attacks. She's had so many. It'll pass."

"I understand," answered Caio, his voice all false kindness. "She always treated me like a son. Poor woman! Her nerves are a wreck."

As this conversation was going on, Ernest was holding Desiderio, helped obligingly by a few of the spiritual assistants serving in the clinic. One of the latter advised that, since Desiderio was so aggressive, he should be put in a cell. Others disagreed. Most of the time since Elyse had been at the sanitarium, they argued, he had been a steadying influence on her and a helpful companion. She had found support and friendship in him. Hearing he might be incarcerated, Desiderio understood that he faced the possibility of losing Elyse, and quickly regained his composure. Ernest tried to reassure the assistants and took the opportunity to introduce Desiderio as a dear brother. He had lost control of himself, Ernest explained, because of some family problems. Ernest, however, was there precisely to help him get rid of his destructive memories.

Apparently satisfied with this explanation, the assistants went their separate ways.

Afterwards, Ernest invited his rival to follow him. They went outside and sat on a large bench in a nearby garden. Desiderio was crying, angry because he had been stopped from giving the lawyer a good thrashing: "Did you see that cad?" He was still explosive, but he looked on Ernest with less cruelty than Ernest was used to from him. "I don't know why I haven't killed him. The man is despicable. First, he murdered a colleague, Tulio Mancini, then he killed my daughter, little by little. And, after stealing everything he could from her, he wants to crush Elyse."

Ernest gave him a sympathetic look and said, "Desiderio, forgive the awful things I've done to you and listen, please. Calm down, for the love of God! I'm not asking this for us, but for the Elyse you love so much. Right now, I won't deny anything you say about me, but let's call a truce. If we're going to deal with the situation, we have to stay calm. I can tell you first that Elyse is near the end of her physical life."

"I had a feeling that is the case," replied Desiderio. He was now much less hostile, and for the first time, showed signs of real understanding and agreement. "But I'll fight like a bull to defend her," he continued. "I'll give her all my energies, my life. My soul is hers, just like the body she breathes in is mine. We live in the same flesh, we think with the same mind."

"Thank God I understood that that's how it has been," Ernest agreed, showing the humility that was a mark of the elevated degree of selflessness he was ac-

quiring. "Since you spoke so plainly at our first meeting," he went on, "I have recognized Elyse had found
in you the support she needs. Believe me, if I wish anything for her today, it's to see her happy next to you.
I'm convinced that she won't last much more than a
few days in the physical body, and today's shock isn't
going to help matters."

"Ah, Caio, the bastard!"

"No, Desiderio—not like this, I beg you. Try to be
patient and more accepting. Aren't rebellion and hate
wearing us out? After I tried to kill you, and thought I
had, I suffered the rest of my earthly life. Guilt wracked
me, and I spent my best years constantly hiding from
myself in the business world. As for you, you've lived
in a wasteland, full of trials and tribulations particularly
reserved for suffering, unrepentant individuals. Why?
Because you haven't forgiven me and our friend
Amancio. Couldn't Elyse's death bed be the place where
our madness ends, where we make peace? Elyse will be
free of her torments. But how about us? What will happen to us, once she leaves her material body if we continue tormenting each other with guilt and condemna-
tion, crime and punishment? She'll leave..."

Desiderio, disturbed at the thought that he and
Elyse might be separated, yelled out impulsively, "Elyse
won't leave my arms. She'll never abandon me—I won't
let her!"

"Desiderio, we can protest against the forces of life
all we want, but it doesn't do any good. God's laws will
be obeyed. Elyse relies on you, but she also loves her

daughter. She believes that Caio has separated her and Vera Celine forever, and so unconsciously she wants to die. Now that she has found out about Caio's less than noble character, her death will come sooner rather than later. The poor soul will go on thinking about death, no doubt, in the hope that she'll find herself with you. But the opposite will happen. Death will put her in a situation exactly opposite to yours. She doesn't have your mental make-up, or your inclination for staying on this plane. Today she resents her future son-in-law. Tomorrow she'll learn to forgive and support him, and to submit herself to the Messengers of the Greater Life through prayer. She has an irritable nature—both of us know that very well. But she doesn't hate anyone, and she's never shown a penchant for revenge."

Desiderio slipped to his knees on the ground . He put his head between his hands and started to cry with greater desperation than ever.

"Forgive, Desiderio. Forgive all of us—even Caio."

"Never, never!"

"I recognize the injustices we carried out against you; I see the nobleness in your heart. Show us who you really are, and listen to me. I thank you for devoting yourself to a woman I didn't know how to make happy and for the love you showed my daughter—the sacrifices you made to take care of her. For all of that, I beg you to extend the vibrations of your mercy and empathy to us, your killers."

"Ernest, Ernest! Why try so hard to reconcile? It's impossible!" He roared these words, as if fighting back new emotions. "Why are you putting all this effort into trying to change me?"

"Desiderio, in the physical world we work specifically with dense matter. We transform stones, metals, lands, waterfalls. Here in the Spirit World we deal in a special way with spiritual forces. We renew souls and consciences, starting with our own. Listen to me. You have to remember that Elyse, just like Evelyn, has many friends in the Higher Planes who'll ask that she be brought there. For the love of Evelyn—and I know she lives in your memory like a guardian angel—improve your attitude. I ask you to start by pardoning us. We need that so much!"

"Evelyn—Evelyn, my daughter." Desiderio spoke the words with a sigh, then broke into sobs. "No, I won't let you drag her into this conversation," he said. "Evelyn must live with the angels! I would gladly suffer in Hell or struggle in the mud, both of which I deserve, if it meant that all she would ever know is happiness in Heaven."

"But what if she comes to meet you one of these days, and pleads our cause? Asks you to support us, pleads for your mercy as our creditor and your debtors?"

Desiderio tried to speak, to break through the barrier of pain burning in his soul. At that moment, however, one of the disincarnate assistants rushed up and interrupted them. He had come to notify them of an unexpected development. At the end of her crisis with Caio, Elyse had fallen into a state of paralysis. A delicate blood vessel had ruptured in her brain. It was a forewarning. Her disincarnation would occur within a few hours.

Hearing this, both spirits forgot themselves and followed the messenger back into the hospital to offer what help they could.

A couple of quick phone calls alerted the alarmed Vera and Serpa of Elyse's turn for the worse. They came to the sanitarium together and found Elyse in agony, but in an atmosphere full of calm and tenderness. The doctor, despite attempting to console and give them hope, was clear in his advice, "All we can do is wait."

Vera Celine, crying, knelt at Elyse's feet, knowing she would never again hear her mother's blessing in this world. Caio, evidently annoyed, looked on and smoked cigarette after cigarette. Nurses came and went, trying to lend a hand. Meanwhile, spiritual helpers formed a magnetic current of support, making sure that Elyse's transition would be fast, and upset her as little as possible. In view of the emergency, Ernest returned home to get instructions from Rivas. At the sanitarium, Desiderio planted himself at the head of the bed, deep in denial and despair.

For another eight hours, Elyse held on, her heart pumping life through a drained and motionless body. As dawn came, she opened her eyes very wide, and tried to fix them on her daughter. There was in them an inexpressible goodbye. Feeling Caio's presence—he stood near the bed staring at her—she closed her heart in a dense cloud of anguish, though in truth her soul held no hatred toward him. Mentally she asked Desiderio to protect and defend her. Holding eagerly to this, her last thought in the carnal envelope, he found enough reason to bind himself to her. He seemed to be absorbing all her energies.

Her mother, Vera felt, was finally surrendering to the great repose. Anxiously she tried, without success, to bring her back. "Mother! Mother! Mother!" she continued pleading.

But from the rigid mouth, there was no answer. Elyse Fantini's head dropped on her pillow; her body had become motionless forever.

Later in the sanitarium's infirmary, the nurse pulled a sheet over her face. Elyse's life, so steeped in difficulties and problems, came to an end as the dawn of a new day broke. Behind the scenes, in the spiritual sphere, however, the plot continued. Tied to the dead woman by the force of her own last wishes, Desiderio, burning with hate, held one of her hands in his own right one, preventing her spirit's departure. Elyse, though half-unconscious, realized that she was still tied to him and at the same time handcuffed to her dead body. All the while she listened to him say over and over that he would never let her go.

Brothers[19] and sisters of Earth, in the midst of the uncertainties of human life, learn to tolerate and for-

---

[19] *Translator's Note: Reflections by the spiritual author.*

give one another. No matter how much you are hurt or slandered, injured or cursed, forget evil and always do good. When your confidence is betrayed or your spirit torn to pieces by the traps of the darkness, turn on love's light, wherever you are. If you are vilified or insulted, even though your intentions are for the best, forget the offenses and forgive the outrages that prepare your heart for the Greater Life.

Sisters, who have suffered injuries to your own flesh and been driven mad by the false promises of smiling torturers who despise you, bless the ones who have destroyed your dreams! Single mothers, banished from homes and hounded into prostitution because you had enough courage not to kill the children growing inside your wombs, anguished mothers, who have so often been denied the right to defend even yourselves, forgive those who persecute you!

Parents, carrying on your bruised shoulders the painful weight of ungrateful children; children, standing up under the physical and mental abuse of insensitive parents; husbands and wives stabbed to the heart by daggers of incomprehension and cruelty, forgive one another!

For those of you who find yourselves beset by ill-meaning spirits, weave compassion and hope around these unhappy beings, incarnate or disincarnate, who torture you! Men and women everywhere in the world, ruined or persecuted, forgive the instruments of your sorrows and tears! When the thought of revenge tempts you, remember the One who told us to love our enemies, pray for those who persecute and torment us!" Remember the

Christ, who preferred being condemned to condemning, because, in truth, those who practice evil don't know what they're doing to themselves!

Be assured that the laws of the true life make no exception, and don't forget that, on the day when you say your final farewells to your loved ones, it is only through the blessings of peace and love and with a clear conscience that you will be able to find your much desired liberation!

Chapter 24

EVELYN IN ACTION

Before the sun rose again, Ernest, Evelyn, and a few friends from the Institute of Spiritual Protection—a small assistance caravan led, at Instructor Rivas's request, by Brother Plotino—had reached São Paulo. The group's aim was to cooperate with spiritual assistants involved in the liberation of Elyse, who was now locked in the prison of her own remains. They were told that Vera Celine had taken her mother's body home, and the group headed on to Vila Mariana.

Evelyn's heart was full of anxiety. She had carried her father's image in her memory for many years, knowing it only through family photographs. Now she was going to see him for the first time, and found herself eager—encouraged by Ernest—to understand and assist him.

They had almost reached the doorstep when Plotino recommended that the group stop. He would go inside alone, he told them, make a quick inspection, and decide what had to be done.

Attended by Vera Celine, who in turn was being looked after by Caio, some neighborhood friends and various spiritual helpers, Elyse was at an impasse. Desiderio held her by one hand, sustaining her with his life force. She was semi-conscious and seemed to be enjoying this strange, new hypnotic state.

Plotino questioned the nurse heading the support group charged with releasing Elyse from her body. In response, the nurse confessed his worst fears. He could force her to leave her body, he said, but he couldn't break through her perfectly lucid thoughts. He could compel her release; but he had no means of isolating her from Desiderio, on whom she had become wholly dependent. Someone would have to intervene with sufficient argumentative powers to persuade Desiderio to change his attitude.

Brother Plotino, a gentle, friendly soul, approached Desiderio and asked his help in liberating Elyse. She needed to be taken to a spiritual colony for recuperation, he said. Desiderio moved around the foot of the bed and drew closer to Elyse. "You fools!" He roared savagely, "You're not going to make me leave. What do you want in this house? She's my woman. No begging or any amount of praying is going to make me let her go. I have experience! I know spirits who don't separate from their bodies. Nobody—positively nobody—is going to take me out of this room!"

"Someone *will* do it, brother Desiderio," said

Plotino, without altering his tone.

"Who? Tell me who!"

Plotino smiled. "God," he said quietly.

Desiderio let out a terrible blasphemy.

Plotino went back to meet with the others. He explained what was going on inside and detailed his plan of action. This was the moment for Evelyn's personal intervention. The rest of the group would continue to pray, in order to help her. She would go in alone and try to bring about her father's renewal. Most likely, he would obey her without hesitation.

Within a few moments, the group's thoughts became concentrated on one objective and one only. Fused into one, aimed only at projecting loving energy, these prayerful hearts, without any theatrics, sent a bright glow of sapphire-like light toward the house's entrance. They had, it seemed, conferred on Evelyn a badge of merit for undertaking this blessed assignment. She herself became bonded spiritually to them; they became her source of equilibrium and support. Like a star transformed suddenly into a woman, she entered the room.

Terrified, Desiderio stared at this apparition and fell to his knees.

Yes, it is she, my daughter, my Evelyn. I've never forgotten her, not even when I found myself immersed in the darkest shadows!

As Evelyn looked at him, she projected a sweet tenderness. Her father, in the light she irradiated, examined and passed judgment upon himself. He saw that he was a convict who had remained, year after year, at the farthest corner of his cell without caring for himself. He was a monster in the presence of an angel, and like a disgraced and beaten dog, he tried to crawl away, to escape.

Evelyn guessed his intention. "Father," she said simply.

Desiderio felt that voice reach into his most vital being. Yes, that word came to him from this beloved daughter—a soul he had given up hope of ever meeting again.

He rose, his knees trembling. Astonishment overcame him, and he burst into tears.

"So it is you—my daughter. God has sent you to ask me for the impossible?"

Evelyn came closer, and put her right hand on his suffering forehead. "Father," she said, "God certainly blesses our meeting. But we, you and I, are promoters not of the impossible, but of reconciliation in His name, our Creator and Father of Mercy."

"What do you want from me, Evelyn?"

"I've come to invite you to be with me. Do you think I haven't dreamt all this time of this moment? I went through my childhood and adolescence talking to your portrait. I married on Earth, and on my wedding day, I pleaded for your blessings in my prayers. And when the Divine Design took my physical body, I cherished the dream of finding you again!"

Desiderio made a gesture of self-pity. "Look what they've made of me, Evelyn," he complained, "the criminals who destroyed us."

"Oh, Father, don't accuse anyone! You've suffered, yes. But suffering is always sacred before God. You've endured difficult tests, yes. But every day shows us a chance for renewal and ascension to a higher destiny."

"In the Divine Dwellings—where you deserve to be—you must have heard that I didn't lose my body by accident."

"Yes, today I know the whole truth."

"So you can't deny that our executioners are the same people. We were robbed by the same bandits! If there's no memory of evil in Heaven, I'll remind you that Amancio Terra, the criminal who set himself up as your stepfather—."

He couldn't go on, he was gasping so hard. Evelyn took the opportunity to clarify the matter. "You won't be upset with me," she said humbly, "if I tell you he always wished me well and respected me as his own daughter. I can't deny that he committed a serious crime against you, before the Divine Law. But I trust that his repentance for that act—which he has been carrying for over twenty years—speaks for itself. Because of it, he has undergone a renewal, and become an honorable man."

"Don't forget that he sent you away from home when you were still a child."

"He sent me to school, Father. He gave me the discipline that protected me from temptations I would otherwise surely have given into during my time in the world. He never hesitated when it came to helping me. He didn't try to stop me from getting married. When I was a child, he used to encourage me to study. He was interested in my grades, and he would reward my efforts with gifts and tenderness only a father could give. He never replaced you in my heart as a father, but I can't be ungrateful to someone who gave me so much. At home, he was the protector of our happiness. I never saw one gesture of disrespect toward Mother from him."

"Don't talk to me about Brigitte. She's evil, that woman."

"Father, don't condemn the one person who united us. What could Mother do? She was still so young, with a baby to take care of—she needed a husband's support. When she accepted Amancio, she didn't deliberately marry the hunter who killed you. She married the friend you yourself brought home one day, someone from happier times she remembered during her days of longing and desolation. Mother always taught me to revere your memory and honor your name."

At these evidences of his daughter's superior understanding, Desiderio, in his self-pity, cried even harder, as if he were searching, somehow, for new reasons to be unhappy.

"Maybe you also know I'm here with the family of another enemy I can't forgive, Ernest Fantini. He tried to kill me; in fact, he was your stepfather's inspiration. This body"—he gestured toward Elyse—"which is alive through my hands, was his wife. He tried to murder me in a fit of jealousy over her. Well, the only thing he did was bring the two of us closer. Brigitte's behavior forced me to leave home. Think what your father has had to endure, Evelyn! She forced me out of my own house after I died, she was so under the influence of my persecutor. So I had to find refuge with someone else. And in the thoughts of this woman, my companion who's dead to this world today, I found sustenance!"

"None of us understand God's plans completely, Father," Evelyn replied. "But aren't we all involved in a network of witnesses to love, even with all our faults and compromises in past lives? I ask Divine Providence to bless our sister Elyse and reward her for the good she has done. As for Ernest Fantini, I have to tell you that he has been a devoted friend to me in the Spiritual Life. He cared for and was kind to me long before he knew I was linked to you. He helped me restore my energies. At every stage of my new path, he has supported me like a brother."

"My dear girl, you look through the eyes of the angels, so you see these rascals as benefactors. But I can't look at human beings from a heavenly viewpoint. I'm a man—an angry man—and nothing more. Besides, I can't believe you feel so generous toward your own killer, this fugitive from jail who sits masked right here before our eyes—Caio Serpa."

"You don't know what you're saying, Father," said Evelyn, even more compassionately. "Caio was a generous guide to me. He helped me understand so much about life and gave me greater confidence in myself. He filled me with dreams of happiness when I was young, and helped me live. I imagined paradise on Earth with him. And if he expected a happiness from me I couldn't give him, is that a reason to condemn him? He assumed debts with Tulio Mancini and he'll certainly pay them in time—that's beyond question. But why reject our loved ones when we find out they're not as happy with us as we thought they were? Don't you think delinquent brothers like Caio are sick and need attention? They're victims of a kind of madness. Why not show them the same understanding and care we would show the victim of an accident? We shouldn't treat a mutilated spirit worse than a mutilated body."

Her father's complaining, however, now became more insistent than ever. "Unfortunately, I don't know how to forgive," he said "Life is crushing me, Evelyn. I feel as if I've been run over by a car and turned into a useless rag."

"Father, don't you see we're all children of God, and depend on one another?"

"I don't! I don't understand why I have to make up with people who beat me into the ground."

"Do you want to move ahead? Be free and happy?"

"Oh, yes!"

"Then, forgive the evil they did to you. Do you ever reflect on the power of time? Time helps us discover the fountain of love that washes away all our faults."

"Time, Evelyn? A clock is a devilish machine to a spirit like me. I suffered yesterday, and the day before yesterday; and I suffer today because I hate three wolves: Amancio, Ernest, and Caio. And I suffer for defending three sheep: Elyse, you, and Vera. I don't count Brigitte—I've pushed her far away from me. Do you know that Vera let herself be seduced by your rogue of a husband?"

"Be kind to them, Father! Let's think the best we can of Vera and Caio. Let's think about the future. Tomorrow, they'll be precious friends, devoted protectors."

"You only see the good in these people. I see the evil that conquers good."

"That's not the point. You cannot see that you are ill and in need of help. The reality is that, just as I do at times, you need to readjust your ideas and feelings. In the beginning, Father, I thought I had been robbed by life as well. Many times I thought Mother and my stepfather were enemies—that they sent me away so I wouldn't interfere with their happiness. But at the colony of rehabilitation where I was taken, I started to see them, by God's mercy, as true friends who'd given me all the support I needed. And then not long ago I again saw Caio, who's more strongly attached to Vera Celine than ever. I was crushed. I considered him the ultimate picture of ingratitude. At the same time I blamed Vera as an intruder who had stolen the treasure of my heart. That heart shriveled up; I was all dry inside. Then the dew of the Infinite Goodness of God visited my poor feelings. Instructors, doctors, nurses, all rich in compassion, taught me the lessons of self-renunciation, and I regained my equilibrium. Caio and Vera, I came to see, are spiritually a brother and a sister. They are as they are, and we are as we are, and God wishes us to love one another. God lets us be as we wish to be! He wants us to go on paying yesterday's debts, so we can have a better tomorrow. God, being all-merciful, sows flowers and blessings all along the path we walk. To understand that is to seek our destiny, and helping others guarantees that we're doing just that. Love doesn't fail. God created us to love without end!"

Desiderio was crying so hard he couldn't respond, so Evelyn continued. "Examine your own thinking. It's obvious that Ernest, despite the inner conflicts that kept him away from home, feels a real affection for Elyse. Because of that, and because of his present discernment, he has given her to you from the bottom of his heart. He knows that, in God's sight, you've been and will continue to be a good companion to her. Then why not, for our part, give Caio the same right to Vera? It would bring him the happiness I couldn't give him, even when I was in the physical world."

"But, Evelyn, isn't this kind of renunciation a form of moral suicide?"

"No, Father. True love raises the level of everything. Today I understand that corrupted feelings can be corrected through reincarnation in the family, which truly is a sacred institution. In it, God lets us embrace as children spirits we couldn't learn to love in other circumstances. One day, our thoughts of love toward one another will be pure and free, like streams that meet underground on Earth, or like the light of stars that shine together in the Milky Way without losing their own magnitude and originality."

She paused for a while—the friends around her remained respectfully silent—then she continued. "Your heart is still surrounded by clouds of grief. You have the power to disperse them, to forge ahead and seek peace. For now, let Elyse leave all her bad memories behind her. Set her free, and the woman you want will belong to you more than ever. Help her rise to new paths, and she'll come back to meet you. Don't keep the person who deserves all your devotion locked up in this dungeon of rotting flesh. Elyse will be grateful to you; and for our part, we solemnly promise you, before the Infinite Mercy of God, that you'll see her again in the place we come from. Both of you will prepare there, with our love, for a new life together. You'll be together again, and happy! Please do as we ask, Father."

"No, no! I'm a sinner. I can't deny it," he yelled, more despairing than ever.

Then the most profound and most poignant moment of the meeting occurred.

Evelyn placed her hands on her father's head, raised her eyes, and prayed: "Oh! God of Kindness! My father and I are the united members of a great spiritual family that is now scattered. Please, All-Merciful One, if it's Your wish, let the two of us become more attuned to each other, let us share the same yearning for redemption."

Her voice, stifled by her pain, died away. As she lowered her head toward her father, tears rolled down her cheeks. They fell onto the upturned face of the unfortunate Desiderio, and in that moment, like rich balm, they transformed his heart.

Desiderio let out a painful moan and, in the grip of

forces he couldn't resist, he immediately let go the hand of the dead woman. Embracing his daughter's feet, he cried out, "Evelyn, Evelyn, take me wherever you please! I trust you. Please put out this fire in my spirit—it has only known how to hate! Help me, Lord! Help me, my Lord!"

Evelyn, helped by the force of her companions in prayer, raised him easily, as if taking a fallen child into her arms. Nurses rushed to aid her; then, like a group of technicians, they released Elyse from her inert body, working rapidly as if to remove her from a useless piece of clothing. Plotino and his collaborators in prayer also entered into the action, helping Desiderio, now semi-conscious, to the transport that would carry him to his new spiritual home.

Someone else had discreetly followed the whole exchange between Evelyn and Desiderio. Instructor Rivas had come to Vila Mariana without warning. His intent was to encourage Evelyn, his pupil at the Institute of Spiritual Protection, through prayer. And she had given such an unforgettable testimony! As soon as he saw her, leading her father toward a more sublime plane, this much-revered teacher, perhaps recalling incidents from his own life, silently turned away from the group, his eyes moist with tears that did not completely leave his eyes.

Meanwhile, once again in the streets, the spirit helpers limited themselves to contemplating the morning sky.
The purple dawn announced perpetual renewal and suggested they praise the Infinite Mercy of God. And so they
prayed silently.

Chapter 25

NEW DIRECTIVES

Desiderio and Elyse were admitted to the hospital, and Ernest and Evelyn returned to São Paulo that same afternoon. They wanted to attend Elyse's funeral and determine how Vera was reacting to her new situation. Having a clearer idea of what the future had in store and how Vera's participation and cooperation would be especially important to their own peace of mind, they felt they needed to give her support, warmth, and tenderness.

Equally vital to their work was seeing Desiderio through in his surrender to their ideals of renewal. They also hoped to secure a wider range of action by readjusting some of Caio's attitudes.

They found Vera Celine with a tear-stained face, looking to her friends and relatives for comfort. Caio, in a taciturn mood, stood at the household helm, barking out orders.

Once the funeral procession was underway, the two

disincarnate visitors and some friends from the spirit realm installed themselves in the family car next to Vera. Arriving at the cemetery, Ernest helped his daughter. Evelyn followed after Caio, who decided he could use some distraction from the events at the gravesite.

He had no desire to watch the service. Under the influence of Evelyn—he had taken her to the grave himself two years ago—he was thinking about her, and unintentionally, seeing her face on the screen of his memory. Not far away, Vera cried in the arms of her friends. Caio meditated gloomily. He remembered the time he had left Evelyn in another cemetery, the Quarta Parada.[20] He reviewed in his mind all the incidents surrounding her death. It had been twilight in Vila Mariana, just as it was now, and the same questions had come to mind. Would life end in a heap of stones and ashes? Where do the dead go, provided there is a life after death? Where would his parents be, who died when he was young? In what heavenly region would he find Evelyn, the woman he had loved without measure as a young man, and whose illness and death had separated them?

Then, while remembering her, another face suddenly appeared before him, that of Tulio Mancini. His heart tightened in his chest. Why had he been so insane as to kill the man? The crime emerged from his memory in its minutest details.

He was determined to stop these thoughts. Yet for

---

[20] *Author's Note: A cemetery in the city of São Paulo.*

some reason he felt bound to the past. He had no idea of Evelyn's presence in spirit next to him, and her part in forcing him to awaken spiritually to these truths.

"Caio, what are you doing with your life?" She asked him gently.

Physically, the question failed to register; but, thinking he was talking to himself, he heard it in the soundchamber of his soul.

"Caio, what are you doing with your life?"

The words of his former wife echoed in the innermost temple of his conscience. *Time is going by*, he thought; *I'm not paying enough attention to what I'm doing*. For what values was he exchanging the legacy of time? In what resources was he investing his health and money? What good were his academic credentials doing him or anyone else? He had killed a friend; and as a husband, he had lacked the courage to be sincerely good to his wife even in her final illness.

His eyes fell inadvertently on Elyse's funeral service, and he wondered what he had really represented to the woman. In fact, where she was concerned, he didn't feel very good about himself. He had always treated her impatiently, harshly, interested as he was in taking her daughter's affection away from her. In the school of life, he realized, his conscience was giving him failing grades. He looked over at Vera, trying to figure out from her expression what was going on inside her.

"Caio, think of your duties. Don't you think it's time you made your relationship to Vera legal?" Evelyn whispered in his soul's ears, "After all, she gives herself to you completely."

Convinced he was talking to himself, Caio silently repeated the question, unaware that Evelyn was listening to his answers. He supposed he was only following a process of self-criticism, and so his soliloquy continued. "Legalize my relationship with Vera? Marry her? Why?" Yes, he'd promised Vera he would marry her and he still liked the idea, but he wasn't about to act on it without scrutinizing the situation more closely. He had been there before, tied down by marriage vows, and he wasn't about to get emotionally involved again, at least not with all those constraints holding him back. Besides, he was a man of the world. He had heard some not very flattering comments about Vera that hardly recommended her as a wife. A number of young men he had spoken to about her had given her a far-from-clean dossier. Why should he give his name to such a woman?

"Caio, who are you to judge?"

Evelyn's question echoed in his soul in the form of a dazzling idea that both touched and frightened him. New appeals rushed in upon him with the impact of truths hitting against the innermost temple of his being.

"Caio, who are you to judge? Aren't you, by your own admission, someone with serious debts before the Law? Why condemn a young woman who made mistakes because as a girl she had no moral guidance to lean on?"

With these admonitions in mind, he continued his self-examination. Would it be fair to leave Vera, now that she was alone in the world? If he did, where would she go? And who was he, Caio Serpa, but a man headed toward middle age who needed someone to help him keep his life on track? He had experienced all kinds of sensual pleasures in his life, but what was he left with at the end of every love affair? This was beginning to look like irresponsibility and self-abuse. What had he gotten from all his wild nights, full of loud boasts yet devoid of meaning, except exhaustion and disillusionment? Up to now, as far as he could remember, he had never helped anyone. He could be affable enough, if circumstances didn't upset him, but he had only to be contradicted in a small point, in any situation, to jump ship and not be bothered any more. Wasn't it time to start getting involved, help someone, be of use to someone? In the beginning, caught up in his game of conquest, he had showered Vera with kindness and tenderness, using all his charms to captivate her. Later, satiated, his interest died down and boredom set in—typical of a man who doesn't know how to love. He couldn't deny, though, that Vera had placed her entire trust in him, and had given herself wholly to him. In the end, she hadn't hesitated to humiliate her own mother, forcing her to follow his orders and put him in control of her financial assets.

Caio received all these arguments from the disincarnate Evelyn, all the while supposing he was their source—rather as if a light bulb (if it had thought) might suppose that it and not the power company was the source of the lamp's light. Still he put up resistance:

"Marry? Get tied down again? Why? Don't I have all the advantages of a married man, and none of the problems?"

But Evelyn's voice kept sounding in his spirit: "Caio, you're the dominant partner in this relationship while Vera Celine plays the submissive role. She will feel a lot more secure in her love for you and be a good and devoted mate if you marry her. At the same time, a real commitment will protect you against future temptations that would lead you to philandering. That has characteristically been a problem for you through your whole love life, hasn't it? Do you think you're over it yet? Wouldn't it be better to guarantee her peace and yours by bringing a little self-discipline into your life? Think about it; imagine yourself in front of your own mother when she was first married to your father. What every man looks for in a wife is the unconditional support of a mother, which he lost when he grew up. What would you think of a man who robbed a girl such as your mother of her purest heart's desires? Would it not stir up all your most protective instincts if you saw her trust betrayed? If you saw her abandoned and forgotten by the very person she had trusted with her life? So why do you talk of being stifled in marriage? These attitudes can only be hurtful and make her need your protection and understanding more and more."

From cautions, Evelyn now changed to thoughts of hope and optimism.

"Think, Caio! Vera didn't trust you with just a small sum of money to invest. You would have far more than you need to raise a family. Think of the wonderful things the future could hold. And listen, whether you believe in God and an afterlife or not, you're still carrying a painful problem around with you—one you haven't been able to get rid of up to now—your guilt over murdering Tulio Mancini. You killed a colleague and that memory is always there. You try to lose the pain of it in pleasure, but that doesn't work. You try to block out those dark images, but they constantly break in on you. But to be a father, taking care of your darling children— wouldn't that be the best compensation you could make on Earth? Marrying Vera will legally put you in possession of assets you could cultivate and add to, so that your children would be guaranteed security and comfort, happiness, a good education, and a new home. Caio! A home, where you can rest, renew yourself, forget, with children who'll mirror you as you were in your young days, and a life with Vera, who will remind you of the refuge you lost in your mother!"

These evocations of peace and new enterprise, which he had never experienced before, brought Caio to tears for the first time in many years.

"Yes, Caio," Evelyn continued, "bathe your heart in tears—tears of hope, joy! Let's trust God and life! The sun that's dying today will be back tomorrow. Think about these stones, these graves in front of you. Everywhere around them there's an explosion of greenery and flowers. They're telling you that death is an illusion, that life triumphs, beautiful and eternal! From another world, the people who love you will be so pleased with your acts of understanding. Tulio will forgive you, Elyse will bless you! Have courage—courage!"

Caio, surprised but incapable of sensing Evelyn's presence, found himself suddenly happy. He felt euphoric, inspired in the secret recesses of his being by a sense of renewal and peace. Like a sick man who has found the right medicine and holds on to it, anxious for a cure, he instinctively decided not to lose the moment, to act on this positive exaltation before it disappeared.

"Let's go," insisted Evelyn. "Let Vera know right now that you'll marry and protect her!"

Then the unexpected happened. Usually obstinate and aggressive, Caio, embraced all the while by Evelyn's spirit, left his retreat, and with a good deal of humility, walked toward the group surrounding Vera. There, with his thoughts united to Evelyn's, he saw his fiancée in a new light. He began, it seemed to him, to love her in a different way. He felt compassion for her in her grief; he realized her loneliness, her genuine need for companionship. Suddenly, he recognized that he too was lonely, and that he needed her dedication and tenderness. In that unforgettable instant, he didn't know for sure whether he wanted her with the impatience of a man or the tenderness of a father.

He approached her, gently took her arm, and told her, intentionally speaking aloud so that her friends would witness his words, "Vera, don't cry any more. You're not alone! Tomorrow, we'll start getting the necessary documents together so we can get married. As soon as possible!"

Vera gave him a significant and appreciative look. As they prepared to leave, the two leaned on each other. Evelyn and Ernest, and a few spiritual friends, paid their last respects to Elyse. They prayed, thanking God especially for the transformation that had just taken place in Caio.

One more important step had been taken on the road toward a better future. With Divine help, Caio and Vera would make a home. Tulio Mancini would come back to Earth, a member of the family of the man who had taken his former life. In this way the Law of Love, which says that in the end hate and revenge will be forever banished from the Work of God, would be satisfied. Later, Elyse would join the family as a much-loved daughter. Caio would find new comfort, become another man who, with Vera's loving care, would see his life extended in happy posterity.

Evelyn, thinking of all this, was unable to stop her cries of jubilation. She still loved Caio, but on another level now. With all her soul, she thanked God for the existence of Vera Celine; she began to admire the woman and wish her well. Vera Celine was willing to render services that she could never repay.

In an ecstasy of happiness, she ran to meet the engaged couple, and before Caio could settle beside Vera in the car, she hugged him gratefully. Full of love purified by the fires of suffering—of heavenly love— she shouted to his heart for the first time, "Caio, my dear! My dear! Be happy, and God bless you!" Then, leaning toward Vera, she kissed her hand with indescribable tenderness. The car moved away, toward home.

For a long time, Evelyn and Ernest remained at the cemetery in prayer. It had been transformed for them into a place of new awareness and happiness. Before they left, the first stars, lanterns of silver light and fire, appeared above them illuminating the path to God.

Chapter 26

AND LIFE GOES ON . . .

C aio and Vera's marriage gave Ernest and Evelyn a new incentive to work harder than ever. Tulio, feeling slightly better after his beloved Evelyn promised her future help, agreed to enroll at the Institute of Reincarnation Services. Immediately he was admitted to one of the restrictive quarters, and gave himself up to all the necessary preparations.

Before he incarnated, Evelyn took him, on a night when Caio was away from home, into Vera's presence, so that he could become more familiar with his future mother. At Vila Mariana he saw Vera sewing and instantly empathized with her, noting her mild features, her agile hands at work, and the serene eyes of someone who has known suffering. He breathed in the tranquillity of the place and pronounced himself delighted.

Evelyn now made a request. She asked him to embrace Vera, to show his esteem for this woman who would bless and protect him, in God's name, as a son.

He did so, not only taking her in his arms, but tenderly kissing her on the forehead.

Vera didn't directly perceive this sign of affection but, for a few moments, she let herself drift into reverie, thinking cheerfully: "How I would love to have a little boy! How I'd love to be a mother!" It was a blessing she fully expected from the All Merciful Who, surely, wouldn't forget her! On the other hand, she knew Caio wanted a son more than anything, so even in her dreams she consciously asked God for a little boy.

These premonitions of motherhood appeared at the center of her soul, bringing her more closely into harmony with Tulio and putting them both on the same wavelength of hope and joy. Both sensed the prelude to an inexpressible happiness. As he was saying goodbye, he asked Evelyn the question she'd been expecting all along: where was his father? Who would he call father? The man of the house was away, she explained quickly, but in due time he would meet him.

It was a discreet answer, knowing as she did that he would be reborn to Caio Serpa. At the same time, according to their plan, he would be totally enthralled by his mother's devotion. This would bring him into close proximity to his old enemy, and through the therapy of forgetfulness, transform his resentment into love.

With so many ongoing developments, Ernest and Evelyn found their time filled with pleasant and wonderful duties. Tulio, Caio, and Vera, in preparation for the future, received constant attention; and their sup-

port for Elyse and Desiderio, who were now hospital-
ized, was tireless. Ernest, renewed by suffering, looked
younger, and Evelyn, changed by her new experiences,
seemed to have matured. It was as if the two had agreed
to readjust their appearances to harmonize their respec-
tive ages. Moreover, they shared the same duties and
similar ideas.

As their association grew deeper and more intimate,
and their progress more apparent, this gradual realign-
ment seemed to appear automatically. It impressed
Ernest greatly. One day he sought Instructor Rivas, and
respectfully asked if it would be possible to know his
past by accessing the memory of his former lives.

The instructor looked at him and said sensibly, "No,
Ernest. It could be done, but I wouldn't recommend it.
In our plan, you and Evelyn have embarked on a long
period of service. You have a great many problems to
solve yet, and much work to do. Desiderio, Elyse,
Amancio, Brigitte, Caio, Vera, Tulio, Evelyn, and you are
part of a group of related spirits. You've been involved
with each other, under God's Law, for many centuries
now. You're all interlocked in a probationary process,
like chemical elements in a hot crucible getting ready
for vital purification. There are other members of this
group too, and in time they'll arrive and participate in
the general victory built on foundations of love, but this
is still far ahead of us. We make up, myself included, a
great family." He then noted with a smile, "Over here
there are thousands of us in the same condition. We
work and struggle for our redemption, and we begin

by perfecting ourselves in the recesses of our own personal world."

"We really have no idea while we're on Earth of all the work we'll be called on to do after death, do we?" Ernest could accept this amazing fact calmly now.

"None. But a worthwhile project has to be well managed. First comes the plan, then the execution. On the physical plane, we imagine life continuing in the spiritual world. In the spiritual world, we imagine ourselves correcting, readjusting, improving, and polishing the very same life on the physical plane. We are travelers from cradle to grave, and from grave to cradle. We're reborn on Earth and into Spirituality as many times as it takes to learn, to renew, to rectify, and to progress, according to the Laws of the Universe, until we reach Perfection. That is our common destiny."

"So perhaps Evelyn and I will be reincarnated in the future from the very ones we're working to bring together now."

"Who knows? It's very likely, since it's obviously natural."

Before Rivas could finish, Ernest broke in, a little timidly, like a young man opening up his heart to his father. "Instructor Rivas, Evelyn and I have been thinking—thinking . . ."

He couldn't finish the sentence. Rivas, seeing his nervousness, did it for him, his words full of good humor. "We know, Ernest. Both of you have been thinking about a future together. An understandable and honest desire, considering how aware both of you are now of the great work of transformation and perfection you'll be presiding over in your spiritual group—and for a long time to come."

"Is there any reason we shouldn't?"

"Absolutely none. Especially now that Elyse and Caio have released you from any commitments."

Ernest, shy as he was, would like to have stayed on this topic, but an assistant from the Institute entered the office with a sense of urgency in his manner. He was looking for Ernest, whose help Evelyn needed. She was getting ready to travel to the physical sphere as part of her work with Vera, who was now in an advanced stage of pregnancy.

In bidding goodbye, Rivas said, pleased, "Don't worry about it, Ernest. We'll think about the subject."

Ernest's and Evelyn's days sped by, full of work. Little by little, they realized how much it was going to take to ensure a relatively easy rebirth for a problematic individual like Tulio. He required constant attention so as to avoid a miscarriage, which would upset the general plan. In thousands of other cases, they discovered, miscarriages weren't an important worry. Spirits suited to the carnal world adjusted to the reincarnation process as easily as putting on a glove. In other instances, the spirits going back to the physical plane were so spiritually elevated that their presence alone kept unwholesome spirits at bay and brought an atmosphere of calm to the mother's mind. Tulio, however, was neither an unconscious individual nor a spiritually aware one. He was neither on the base of the mountain nor on its summit. He was a man of middling culture and virtues; and if he showed a keen sensibility now, it was only because of his need to improve himself as the result of the debts he had acquired in past lives.

Any disturbance in Vera's daily life caused him to be irritable; the smallest difficulty left him indisposed. During the arduous treatment for his critically watched return to Earth, he was kept in therapeutic sleep. On Earth, this return is called *pregnancy*—as if pregnancy were an insignificant and similar occurrence for every reincarnating soul, with comparable repercussions for the mother. It is important to recognize, however, that the therapeutic sleep of the spirit, along with its fetal development, is characterized by a variation of degrees, not always bordering on total unconsciousness.

Designs and undertakings aimed at benefiting Tulio increased until the day his first wailings were heard in the cradle. Vera was in ecstasy and Caio full of emotion, marveling at their little son. Tulio had pierced the great barrier between the two worlds. From here on, he would require care of another kind.

This gradual execution of their program brought Ernest and Evelyn a large measure of happiness and satisfaction. Soon they were involved with the next task: Desiderio's return to the physical plane.

First, following the Institute's plan, it would be necessary to install him at Amancio's home in the south of the state of São Paulo. Ernest and Evelyn went for preparatory interviews; they listened to propositions and debates. Desiderio Santos asked, demanded, and complained. Basically, it was impossible to tell him the whole truth concerning his near future; otherwise, he would have been filled with unjustified doubts or simply not have given much thought to it, treating it as irrelevant. He needed to know how imperative it was that he take on a new physical body. He was promised that Elyse would follow him, after some time, and that they would meet again on Earth. However, he was forbidden information about the home where this new opportunity would take place. True, he deserved the blessing of re-incarnation. But he couldn't be allowed to complicate or debase the situation, which after all had been granted by authorities on the Superior Plane, always wise and generous. Above all, it was necessary that he, Amancio, and Brigitte come to terms with each other, and receive, through forgetfulness of the past, the light of reciprocal love. It was in this way alone that they could consolidate their merits before the Divine Law.

Desiderio, however, wasn't easy to satisfy. He blocked resources and claimed rights. In these quarrels Evelyn, helped by Ernest, tried her best to help him, to gain as much of his esteem, acceptance, endorsement, and love as possible.

Then, precisely one year after Elyse's disincarnation, and when Tulio Mancini, in his new re-birth, was about two months old, Desiderio ended his conditional demands for returning to earth. There was, however, one request: he wanted to see Elyse and to talk to her, alone, so they could make plans for their future.

This request was sent to Rivas, who approved it, and Desiderio was taken to Elyse's room. Her mind was now completely clear, and she was recovering peacefully. The two of them, secluded, soon began an intimate conversation. It was a *tête-à-tête* that lasted ten consecutive hours. What they said to each other in that first and last pre-incarnation meeting in the Spirit World is not known. But something unforgettable did happen. Desiderio returned to his own room with a new light in his eyes. All his resentments and questioning had disappeared. He became, from then on, patient and polite.

At the same time, Elyse asked Evelyn's help in getting admitted to an educational institute. She wanted to rehabilitate herself, to learn as much as possible about the problems of the soul before she took on her new earthly body. She was then told she would start her next life in three years and, protected by their spiritual mentors there, would again meet Desiderio. With this news, her desire to learn increased. She became eager to prepare and improve herself, aware that the values achieved in the spiritual realm meant greater support and assistance for anyone who observed them. Delighted, Evelyn agreed. Thus, it was arranged that, for three years prior to her return—to her own previous home as the Serpas' daughter—Elyse would go to a school suitable to her needs. She was taken on under Evelyn's tutelage. The latter would take full responsibility for her—another sign that Evelyn's character and merit were being increasingly noticed in the Institute, where she had learned to dedicate herself and serve. Who can measure God's power in performing miracles of love?

In preparation for his incarnation, Desiderio was taken to the cabinets of restriction. The authorities had already decided that no good could come of his knowing beforehand the conditions of his rebirth. Knowing he would be an abandoned child might very well cause him to want a deeper look into his past, might have driven him to attempt a complete revision of the previous lives that had earned him his upcoming trial. Immersing him in advanced memory processes, it was decided, would be counterproductive. Happily though, after his interview with Elyse, Desiderio had become calmer, more confident, more accepting of the promises made to him. There was another consideration as well. Rivas and his associates saw his return to live with Amancio and Brigitte as a valuable time saver. Thanks to Divine Providence, Amancio and Brigitte would have no need to wait for him in future reincarnations.

Next, Instructor Rivas asked Ernest and Evelyn to establish contact with the woman who would be Desiderio's biological mother. They were to help her in her upcoming pregnancy as much as possible, then make sure Desiderio arrived safely at the Terra's household.

Among the Institute helpers and workers presently living in Brigitte's neighborhood, one woman accepted the task of giving birth to him, despite her general poverty.

Evelyn and Ernest got some quick information about her. She was young, the wife of a farm worker dying of tuberculosis, and she had four other children with pressing needs. Mariana, as she was known, was herself in poor health, and would shortly contract her husband's illness. This was a serious concern because the type of tuberculosis was often fatal. Both she and her husband were ending a valuable cycle of regenerative trials on Earth, and neither would remain in the flesh much longer. Desiderio would be their last child before disincarnation.

To Ernest and Evelyn, raised to the position of guardians, would also fall the task of creating the circumstances whereby the newborn Desiderio would enter the Terra home as an adopted son.

Late one night on the physical plane, Mariana in an out-of-body occurrence during her regular sleep, was escorted by a messenger to a room where Rivas, Ernest, and Evelyn were waiting for her.

She couldn't have presented herself in a simpler manner.

Seeing these benefactors, she stopped before Rivas, and with all the clarity she was capable of and mesmerized perhaps by his wise and gentle gaze, she knelt down and asked his blessing. The instructor, visibly touched by her simple gesture, put his hand on her head and asked Jesus to protect her. Then he said, "Please, get up, Mariana, we have something to talk about."

She rose and took a seat. Rivas introduced her to Evelyn and Ernest, stressing Evelyn so that Mariana might better remember her image once she returned to the physical body, "This is the sister who'll look after you in your next pregnancy, Mariana. Please try and remember what she looks like."

The woman looked at Evelyn, and took an immediate liking to her. "Angel of God, have mercy on me," she begged.

Evelyn touched, her eyes wet,—corrected her. "Mariana, I'm not an angel—only your sister."

Mariana, her body at rest in the material world and now spiritually very distant from her earthly home, was overjoyed at this new prospect of being useful. She turned to Rivas, with whom she had had previous meetings, and said, like a respectful daughter, "Father, I'll obey God's wishes and will have one more son. But I need your protection. My husband Joachim is weaker, sicker. I wash clothes and iron for other people, and work as much as I can, but I make very little. I have four children to take care of. And then—I don't know if you know it, but the rain pours into our shack, and the walls are so cracked that the wind cuts straight through them. Joachim's getting worse; he coughs a lot. Oh, I'm not complaining, Father; I'm asking for your support."

"Don't be afraid, Mariana," Rivas reassured her. "God never deserts us. Your children will be taken care of, and very, very soon you and Joachim will have a bigger house."

"Then I put my trust in God and in you," Mariana exclaimed.

In his last remark the instructor was in fact referring to the couple's approaching disincarnation, after which, because they genuinely merited it, they *would* have a new home—only this one would be in the spiritual kingdom. Mariana, though, had no way of knowing this.

She returned now, helped by Ernest and Evelyn, to the wind-battered old house, and reentered her body. As she did so, her heart beat faster with joy than it ever had . "Joachim! Joachim," she called, shaking her husband. He awakened, startled, mumbling.

"I've just had a dream," Mariana continued. "I met this old man—I've seen him a few other times in my dreams—and he told me we're going to have another baby!"

"Is that all?"

"And a big house."

Joachim laughed. Then, not realizing the truth in his words, he said, "Ah, Mariana! A big house, is it? Only if it's in the *other world!*"

The spiritual visitors smiled. Evelyn, knowing how little time Joachim had left on Earth, was touched. She said a prayer, asking the Lord to give the man strength. Then she promised herself she wouldn't rest until she had brought Mariana and her mother Brigitte together. Brigitte's generosity would greatly relieve the couple's last days in this house, which was so full of suffering.

Two days later, Evelyn, with Ernest's help, and with permission from the higher authorities, took up residence in her stepfather's home. Immediately she began influencing her mother's heart, leading her thoughts toward the goals she and Ernest had planned. She gave Brigitte dreams of the baby who would soon be coming to her arms; filled her heart with feelings of charity and hope, and suggested inspirational readings; stirred conversations between Brigitte and her husband on their future, which God would lighten with the presence of a little adopted son. In response, for the first time in the manor house, Brigitte and Amancio started regular prayers together—Brigitte, under her daughter's sweet influence, managed to convince her husband to join in her bedtime devotions. To her amazement and his own, Amancio had agreed good-naturedly. With equal astonishment, Amancio found his wife suddenly filled with love for her neighbors, and, as a man devoted to the practice of brotherhood himself, he encouraged these altruistic outpourings.

They planned and planned. If God were to send them an adopted son, they'd give him all the love still left in their hearts; they would pay close attention to his inclinations so as to lead him to suitable work; and when he grew up, they would fulfill a long held dream. They would move to the city of São Paulo and there see that the boy got a good education. In this they would ask the help of Caio, their former son-in-law who had just remarried and remained a friend, despite writing them only on special occasions.

If they were to have a little son!

So the designs of these two hearts, so mature in experience, appeared to them always livelier and more beautiful.

Four months passed by as they made all these plans. Then, on a sunny morning, as the older couple was having a serious talk about helping the neighborhood's poor mothers, Mariana, who lived about two-and-a-half miles away, knocked at the door. She had been led there spiritually by Evelyn, who had come with her.

Brigitte, informed of their visitor by a servant, came to attend to the matter. Immediately, Evelyn threw her arms around her mother, and thereafter Brigitte listened sympathetically to her caller.

Mariana was begging for work. Then, in her sad voice, she told Brigitte something about herself. She had gotten pregnant again, despite having four children already. She had no financial resources. Her husband was sick.

Brigitte, without quite understanding the motives for her compassion, gave the woman some money and promised to visit her in person as soon as her husband came home from work.

Evelyn's heart filled with joy and confidence.

That evening Amancio didn't haggle over his wife's request. The two of them made their way to Mariana's squalid shack, looked over the situation, and took immediate steps to move the family to a small, comfortable house on their farm. Joachim had finally found all the help he'd hoped for before his fifth child was born, and with that, he returned to spirituality, blessing his benefactors.

Mariana, weak for a long time, now became seriously ill. She appealed to her relatives for help, though they were almost as poor as she, and gave them her four children in anticipation of her coming death. This deepening crisis astounded Brigitte. She grew closer to this poor woman in need, and soon brought her into her own house.

It was there that Desiderio, reincarnated, opened his eyes on a new earthly life.

Convinced she had done her last and sacred duty, Mariana put her baby in the arms of her protector, and five days later passed away. Spirit friends came to welcome her, and at the same time to bless her little one. At the Terra household, full of flowers, emotions were mixed, composed as they were of farewells and greetings for the new arrival, of sadness over one death and joy over another life. Brigitte cried and laughed, and Amancio pondered, touched by these uplifting emotions and ideas.

Ernest and his companion Evelyn sent up a prayer of joy and gratitude at Providence's mercy, and noted, in delight, that as much as for Mariana in her coffin as for Desiderio in his cradle, God had sent the blessing of a new day.

During the night, a transport, in the form of a shimmering star, dropped off Ernest and Evelyn in the city they now called home. As soon as they arrived, they went straight to the Institute of Spiritual Protection. There warm and loving friends threw flowers over them. Lamps of many-colored lights surrounded the place, bathing it in bursts of beauty. The house was celebrating. Here were two workers who had learned, with devotion and humility, how to take the first steps toward building a blessed future.

Surrounded by assistants, Rivas greeted them at the entrance. Then, taking them by the arms, as if they were his own children, he raised his eyes to the sky and prayed, "Lord Jesus, bless your servants, who today consecrate themselves one to the other in sacred union. Enlighten them more and more in their desire for Your kingdom, through which they have managed, by self-sacrifice, to forget hardships and the offenses against them, so that they could help their companions along the way, even when those companions pierced their hearts! Teach them, oh Master, that happiness is a condition built gradually over time and that marriage must be realized again and again—every day—in the intimacy of a home. Only then, in fountains of mutual tolerance, will our defects disappear and our souls find perfect union in Your presence, through the splendor of eternal love!"

The instructor's prayer ended, and Ernest looked at Evelyn, whose face was streaked with tears.

From above, a shower of little blue garlands, like radiant and ethereal sapphires, rained down on them. It was a sign to the happy couple: the Superior Planes approved of their commitment. From the hidden recesses of the landscape soft melodies rose up. With them came words of confidence affirming, in the Knowledge of the Universe, God's everlasting Mercy in the life that, everywhere, continues on, forever more beautiful, full of splendor, sanctified by work, and flooded with light.

Francisco C. Xavier

CHICO XAVIER

Francisco Cândido Xavier, the famous Brazilian medium known affectionately in Brazil and throughout Latin America as Chico Xavier, was born in the city of Pedro Leopoldo, state of Minas Gerais, Brazil, on April 2, 1910. His formal education is basic: he completed only elementary school. Thereafter, at the age of fourteen, he started working full time to help support his family. He retired in 1958 after working for thirty years as a clerk typist for the local government.

Through his amazing paranormality, spiritual authors have dictated works covering a vast range of subjects: from poetry to historical romances to scientific tomes. His first book, published in 1932, was a collection of poems by deceased great masters; it created a true revolution in the literary circles of Brazil and Portugal. However, his greatest contribution, a new vision of Christianity, came through the series of books authored by Emmanuel, who produced historical romances, and André Luiz, who wrote of the life after life. In addition to his work as a medium, Chico has dedicated his life to Jesus, and through his immense charitable work has become known and respected throughout the world among all the religious schools. He was recommended for the Nobel Peace Prize in 1989.

Despite having channeled more than 400 books since 1927, and being the most published author in Brazil today, in worldly terms he is not a wealthy man. From the start he has ceded all copyright to his books to charitable organizations. He leads a very simple life, living on the meager Social Security benefits he earned from working as a civil servant. Yet, measured in terms of the love and respect tens of millions of people in Brazil and all over the world have for him, he can be considered an extremely wealthy individual indeed.